SANDISON'S
SCOTLAND

SANDISON'S
SCOTLAND

A Scottish Journey

with

Bruce Sandison

BLACK & WHITE PUBLISHING

First published 2011
This edition first published 2012
by Black & White Publishing Ltd
29 Ocean Drive, Edinburgh EH6 6JL

1 3 5 7 9 10 8 6 4 2   12 13 14 15

ISBN: 978 1 84502 421 5

A CIP catalogue record for this book is available from the British Library

Typeset by Ellipsis Digital Ltd, Glasgow
Printed and bound in Denmark by Nørhaven

For Ann

"In her eyes I see the kindness of all ages"

Contents

Preface

This is a book about the land I love, about its people, mountains and moorlands and wild places. Most of the stories that appear here first saw the light of day in America by courtesy of my friends Neill and Lynn Kennedy Ray in their publications *Scottish Life* and *The Highlander*. Over the years, many Scots, often through circumstances beyond their control, left their native land to seek a new life overseas. They took with them little other than the strong beliefs and traditions that have made Scotland a byword for decency throughout the world.

The majority of the places visited in my travels are in the far north of Scotland because that is where my wife, Ann, and I have lived for the last thirty years, formerly in Caithness and presently in the small village of Tongue on the north coast of Sutherland. However, I was born and brought up in Scotland's capital city, Edinburgh, Auld Reekie, and I have warm memories of my days there and of expeditions from Edinburgh to the surrounding areas; the splendid Trossachs, the stormy Debatable Lands of the south west and amongst gently rolling Border hills.

Along the way, I have met many people who made my journeys memorable – courteous, considerate, kind and unfailingly welcoming. I have visited places that are the essential adjuncts in the shaping of Scotland's story, from croft to castle, ragged cliff to calm harbour. Together, they make us what we are, a nation at peace with its own identity, proud of its past and confident about its future. And today, for the first time in more than 300 years, we are governed by a Scottish parliament led by the political party that has devoted its lifetime to achieving full independence for Scotland. Could that time be now?

Whatever, I am just happy that I was born a Scot and have had the great privilege of growing up in this wonderful land, and of exploring and discovering the ethos which makes my country so special. My own ethos is pretty well summed up in words from John Barbour's (1320–1395) magnificent poem, "The Bruce": "A noble heart may haif nane ease, na ellis nocht that may him please, gif freedom failye." For everything that Scotland has given me, I am enduringly grateful.

Bruce Sandison

Foreword
Lady Fiona Armstrong-MacGregor

He's a Sandison, and a MacGregor, and I who am married to the chief of Clan Gregor cannot fail to like that. As you start to read, the infamous Rob Roy and the land he rampaged through leap from the pages.

My first meeting with Bruce was not in MacGregor country, in the Trossachs, but on a very wild Highland hill loch. It was more than twenty years ago and we were in search of brown trout. They were moving fast and furious but he carefully guided our rods to tantalising rises and made tiny feathery flies skit enticingly across the water. I was a fledgling angler and for me, he brought the world of fishing to life.

But Bruce is more than an expert angler: a first-class travel writer, a perceptive people-watcher, a hearty hill walker and a scintillating story-teller. He's one of the great exponents of Scottish life and now some of his best work has come together in this un-put-downable collection of tales.

From the heated passion of the Kirkwall Ba' Game, to the solitary and wind-whipped Seal Island, from mighty Edinburgh Castle to the elusive Berwick trolls, Bruce takes us from remote communities to the heart of big cities. Scotland is in his blood and with a pipe-tune named after him, he goes in search of bag-piping experts in Ross-shire.

Later, on a wild whisky tour, he brings to life the story of Macbeth and the three witches on the moor. At Ballindalloch, he finds out about the "doddies", the hardy Aberdeen Angus breed so loved by the late Queen Mother, and learns how the ghost of General James Grant stalks the castle corridors. The old warrior didn't just fight. He never stopped eating and became the fattest man in Britain.

Another man who liked his food and drink was Winston Churchill and as Bruce examines the Scottish Regiments, he reminds us that this famous bon viveur was one of their best-known soldiers. "Although an Englishman, it was in Scotland that I found the best things in my life – my wife, my constituency and my regiment," the war-time Prime Minister said.

We find out how hard life was, and still is, for the crofters of Assynt and, after a lifetime of cooking, I finally realise that a "skink" means soup, that old Scots' favourite of smoked haddock and potato, and it comes from Cullen. And did you know that according to Gaelic verse, the humble hazelnut was the source of all knowledge? From lairds to locals, we hear their stories. There is regret. There are the Clearances and there's the fishing port where you'll now find more yachts than fishing boats in the harbour.

"September is a good-to-be-alive month in the far north of Scotland," he tells us and we sense the dramatic wildness of Wester Ross, "as mountain and moorland resound to the roar of rutting stags and the hills are purple clad with heather." Or, "I stumbled into the shelter of the summit cairn, amazed by the wild landscape that lay before me, wave after wave of mountain crests guarding a blessing where all things were possible and all things equal." I love it! As Rob Roy MacGregor said, "My foot is on my native heath." Bruce MacGregor Sandison's is certainly on his.

Lady Fiona Armstrong-MacGregor

1.
The Trossachs, Clan Gregor Country

Ben Venue (729m) towers above Loch Katrine in the bristling heart of the Trossachs. As I climbed toward its twin peaks, I felt a complete sense of belonging. I was the hill and the rocks about me were my soul. I encompassed time and space. Wind screamed across the ridge. For a moment, I held eternity in my arms. Shivering, I stumbled into the shelter of the summit cairn, amazed at the wild landscape that lay before me; wave after wave of mountain crests guarding a blessing where all things were possible and all things equal.

The Trossachs command a special place in my mind. Not only for their supreme beauty, but also because of the central role they have played in Scotland's story. This is the domain of Clan Gregor, "the children of the mist", robbed of their rightful heritage by their rapacious Campbell neighbours. This is the land of Rob Roy MacGregor (1671–1734), the most famous and redoubtable of his clan. On the plinth of his statue in the town of Stirling are written the words, "My foot is on my native heath, and my name is Rob Roy MacGregor."

My grandmother, Jean MacGregor, was born in Callander by the banks of the tumbling River Teith and I carry her surname with pride. My own mother used to recount, proudly, that she was chosen to sing Clan Gregor's historic song, "MacGregor's Gathering" at a concert in the Usher Hall, Edinburgh, in the early 1920s. As a boy at the Royal High School of Edinburgh, I was thoroughly embroiled in the battles of Otterburn and Bannockburn and immersed in the romantic history of my native land. Sir Walter Scott (1771–1832), "the wizard of the north", was a former pupil and through his writing, Scott, more than anyone else, brought international fame to the Trossachs and to those who called it home. Sir Walter also wrote the words of the song my mother sang:

MacGregor's Gathering

The moon's on the lake, and the mist's on the brae,
And the Clan has a name that is nameless by day;
Then gather, gather, gather Grigalach!
Gather, gather, gather Grigalach!

Our signal for fight, that from monarchs we drew,
Must be heard but by night in our vengeful haloo!
Then haloo, Grigalach! Haloo, Grigalach!
Haloo, haloo, haloo, Grigalach!

Glen Orchy's proud mountains, Coalchuirn and her towers,
Glenstrae and Glenlyon no longer are ours;
We're landless, landless, landless, Grigalach!
Landless, landless, landless, Grigalach!

But doom'd and devoted by vassal and lord,
MacGregor has still both his heart and his sword!
Then courage, courage, courage, Grigalach!
Courage, courage, courage, Grigalach!

If they rob us of name, and pursue us with beagles,
Give their roofs to the flame, and their flesh to the eagles!
Then vengeance, vengeance, vengeance, Grigalach!
Vengeance, vengeance, vengeance, Grigalach!

While there's leaves in the forest, and foam on the river,
MacGregor despite them, shall flourish for ever!

Come then Grigalach, come then Grigalach,
Come then, come then, come then Grigalach!

Through the depths of Loch Katrine the steed shall career,
O'er the peak of Ben Lomond the galley shall steer,
The rocks of Craig-Royston like icicles melt,
Ere our wrongs be forgot, or our vengeance unfelt!
Then gather, gather, gather Grigalach!
Gather, gather, gather Grigalach!

By 1603, the lawlessness of Clan Gregor had become so notorious that James VI proscribed the clan, the consequences of which turned out to be very unpleasant indeed. His edict described them as: "that wicked race of lawless luminaries, callit the MacGregor." Henceforth they were to be pursued and hunted like animals. A reward was offered for the head of every MacGregor delivered to the laird; families were encouraged to betray their own people with promises of pardon; women were branded on the forehead; children were sold as little better than slaves to Lowland and Irish cattle dealers. Even the use of the name "MacGregor" was proscribed.

My wife, Ann, and I have experienced the sense of terror that these people must have felt because it still lingers to this day in the corries and glens in the Trossachs hills and mountains. Some years ago, we were walking to the south of Loch Tummel, heading to fish for trout in little Loch a'Chait, a hard tramp uphill from Lick. It was a hot morning with the sun beating down relentlessly and we found the going hard. Eventually, we arrived at a small, damp glen, peat and heather-filled, where insects hummed in the still air.

I was halfway across the floor of this glen when Ann came running past; when I say running, I mean as fast as she could stumble over the uneven ground, pack on her back, carrying her fishing rod. Her face was white with fear and she kept saying, almost whispering: "Quick, quick, get out of here, get out of here. Something terrible has happened." Without pausing, she hurried on and although I called after her, she didn't stop until she had reached the other side and scrambled up the rocky gully to the top.

When I caught up, Ann was still very distressed and I asked what on earth was wrong. She calmed down and told me that she had a sudden impression, walking across the glen, of women and children in great danger; nothing else, but a terrible feeling that women and children were about to be harmed. It was then that I decided to learn more about what had happened to the "Children of the Mist" during their years of persecution and found an amazing possibility.

Often, before the arrival of the hunters, the clansmen were warned that they were on the way. The first thing the men did, upon receiving this news and before fending for themselves, was to move their women and children to safety, generally into a secret corrie in the hills. But sometimes these hiding places were found and I think that Ann and I had stumbled into one of these hiding places where the women and children had lain, trembling with fear, listening to the sound of their approaching persecutors.

Some years later, talking to the owner of the estate upon which Loch a'Chait lies, he told me that neither he nor the members of his family ever visted the glen that Ann and I had passed through. He could give me no reason why, but said that they felt intensely uncomfortable there and always avoided it.

Rob Roy MacGregor lies asleep in the old churchyard on the Braes of Balquhidder at the east end of glorious Loch Voil. At his side lie his wife Mary, his second son Coll and his youngest son Robin Oig. Whilst Rob Roy died, surprisingly, peacefully in his bed, his son Robin met an altogether harsher fate. Convicted of kidnapping the twenty-year-old Jean Kay from Edinbilly near Balfron in Stirlingshire and forcing her to marry him, Robin paid the price of his crime on the gallows in Edinburgh on 14 February 1754.

Loch Lomond marks the western boundary of the Trossachs and visitors, to gain entry, sailed from Luss across the loch to Inversnaid on the east shore. Dr Johnson and the inevitable James Boswell (also a former pupil of the High School in Edinburgh) passed this way during their famous Highland tour. After enjoying the hospitality of Sir James Colquhoun of Luss and of the novelist Dr Tobias Smollet, Boswell noted: "The civility and respect which we found at every place, it is ungrateful to omit, and tedious to repeat."

William Wordsworth and Samuel Taylor Coleridge, accompanied by Wordsworth's sister Dorothy, also trekked this way in 1803. At Inversnaid, Wordsworth noticed the woman that inspired his poem "To a Highland Girl": "Sweet Highland Girl, a very shower of beauty is thy earthly dower." She was the daughter of the ferryman. Further along his journey, Wordsworth encountered another Highland beauty that prompted him to write one of my favourite poems, "The Solitary Reaper": "Behold her single in the field, yon solitary Highland lass, reaping and singing by herself, stop here or gently pass."

Inversnaid was a less peaceful place prior to the arrival of the literati, entirely due to the activities of Clan Gregor. Their exploits involved the removal of everything and anything not securely nailed down, including cattle, cash goods and chattels. In an effort to subdue the clan, the government built a fort there. But as soon as the fort was completed, the Macgregors attacked and burned it to the ground. As soon as the fort was rebuilt, the Macgregors, led by Rob Roy's nephew, attacked again and destroyed the fort.

Inversnaid was rebuilt for the third time and on this occasion command was given to a nineteen-year-old Lieutenant, James Wolfe, who later met his fate in 1759 at the Battle of the Plains of Abraham outside Quebec in Canada. Wolfe set about his Inversnaid duties with his customary efficiency, sending regular reports to his superior, General Bland, at Stirling Castle. Wolfe never liked either Scotland or its inhabitants, claiming that they were "better governed by fear than favour".

But when the Duke of Cumberland ordered him to shoot a wounded Highland soldier after the Battle of Culloden (1746) because he had looked at him, Wolfe refused to do so, offering to resign his commission instead.

When Walter Scott visited Inversnaid, the fort was still standing, but the soldiers were gone and the door was locked. A retired pensioner was in charge and he was busy working at a small crop of barley. Scott asked him if he could look around the fort and was told that he would find the key under a stone by the door.

The road from Inversnaid climbs past Loch Arklet to reach Stronachlachar on the shores of Loch Katrine. Thereafter, this road, which winds around the loch, is closed to motor vehicles but offers the possibility of a memorable ten-mile walk back to the Pier at the east end of Katrine. Along the way, you will find Rob Roy's birthplace at Glengyle at the foot of Meall Mor (747m). The initials "GM" and the date 1704 are carved on the lintel above the door. Rob Roy's mother is buried in the little graveyard here.

A mile or so west from the Pier is Brenachoile in the Gartney Forest. I never pass this way without paying my respects to Dr Archibald Cameron, brother of Cameron of Lochiel, "out" with Bonnie Prince Charlie during the 1745 Rebellion. The doctor's only crime was tending the wounded after the slaughter of Culloden. He was eventually captured, hiding at Brenachoile, branded a traitor and hanged at Tyburn in 1752.

The eastern boundary of the Trossachs enfolds the lovely Lake of Menteith, graced by the Island of Inchmahome with its thirteenth-century Augustinian priory. During the summer months, a ferry plies between Port of Menteith and the island. As a child, the future Mary, Queen of Scots, found sanctuary on Inchmahome before being hurried off to safety in France – beyond the avaricious grasp of King Henry VIII of England, who was determined that she should be betrothed to his sickly son, Edward.

As I walk the paths that she walked, I sometimes believe that I can hear her infant laughter, but remember with sadness the tragedy of her later life. Poor luckless Mary never stood a chance. Even today, we Scots tend to be wary of clever women but in those days, to be young, female, tall, beautiful, witty, talented and intelligent, and a Queen, was like writing one's own death warrant. The enduring shame of Scotland's lairds is that they connived in her downfall and judicial murder.

But it is hard to be somber for long in the Trossachs. Everywhere you look, around every corner and over every hill, heart and mind are ensnared. A lifetime's joy lives here. I remember one warm evening drifting over the calm surface of Loch Lubnaig, trout fishing in "Bonnie Strathyre", watching a bewhiskered otter splashing in the shallows and seeing the peak of Ben Vorlich (985m) covered in the fire of the setting sun.

And further back, as a boy sheltering from a storm on the shores of Loch Ard, I remember watching huge raindrops making the surface of the loch boil, whilst my father wrestled with the intricacies of an old paraffin stove to boil water to make tea. I remember white-foam-filled rivers urgent with leaping salmon hurrying to their ancient spawning grounds; the autumn scent of heather and the roar of stags on the hill; deciduous woodlands burnished brown and gold, waiting for winter, their branches sparkling with diamond crystals of frost; the first sprinkling of snow on the high tops.

Most of all, I treasure the memory of that singular moment on the windy summit of Ben Venue where I found such peace and content: "Now turn I to that God of old, who mocked not any of my ills, but gave my hungry hands to hold, the large religion of the hills." Get there if you can to the land of Clan Gregor and you will find there all that is finest in this land I love.

2.
The Kirkwall Ba' Game

On New Year's Day in Kirkwall a crowd of young and not so young men waited impatiently on Broad Street in front of St Magnus Cathedral for the start of the 2005 Ba' Game. At the Market Cross, west of the entrance to the old red-sandstone building, veteran Ba' player Ian Smith proudly held aloft a hand-made, brown and black patterned leather, cork-packed ball, which was the object of everyone's rapt attention. As the hands on the face of the clock reached one and the hour struck, Ian flung the ball into the midst of the waiting hoard.

Bedlam ensued as a forest of finger-wide human hands rose to catch the ball. When it was caught, it immediately disappeared into the centre of the throng. Several hundred determined and seemingly deranged men formed themselves into two opposing groups, shoving, heaving and shouting encouragement to those in the middle of the massive scrum. The traditional New Year's Day Men's Ba' game, played between the Uppies and the Doonies, was under way.

This is a fierce, hard-fought, no-holds-barred battle. It is played through the streets of the town, as it has been for over two centuries. To win, the Doonies must immerse the ball in the cold waters of the harbour, whilst the Uppies must touch the ball against the wall at Mackinson's Corner where New Scapa Road, Main Street and Junction Road meet. The game may last for less than an hour, or all day and well into the night. It only ends when one or other of the opposing sides reaches their goal and the single rule is that there are no rules.

The game is as demanding for spectators as it is for the players. Nothing stands in the way of those trying to move the Ba' through the narrow streets of the town. Often, because of the number of men in the scrum, the exact location of the Ba' is unknown. Is it in the pack or has somebody spirited it away? It is also difficult for visitors to identify who is an Uppie and who is a Doonie because the players don't wear distinguishing colours. In truth, the whole affair appears to be a near riot and as such, the authorities, to whom all riot is an anathema, have often tried to "civilise" the event but to no avail.

An imaginary line, drawn through Kirkwall and at right-angles to the Market Cross, divides the town. If you were born to the south of the line you are an Uppie and from "Up-the-Gates". Those born north of the line are Doonies, from "Down-the-Gates"; the word "gates" coming from the Old Norse "gata" meaning road. Team members are also known as being either Earl's Men (Doonies, from the old part of Kirkwall) or Bishop's Men (Uppies, from the newer part). These titles remind us of ancient quarrels between the church and Orkney's ruling earls, when, in times of strife, each side depended for support upon their servants.

Today, place of birth is less relevant, given that most children are born in the Balfour Hospital. The hospital is in Uppie territory and as such, Uppies would always outnumber Doonies and always win. Boys now usually adopt the side that their fathers played for. An exception to this rule is Uppie Jim Cromarty, another Ba' stalwart and Ba' Committee member; Jim's brother John was born at home, in Doonie territory, whilst Jim himself was born in the Balfour, making him an Uppie. Remarkably, both have won a Men's Ba', unique in the annals of the game: Jim wining an Uppie Ba' in 1983, John a Doonie Ba' in 1988.

Newcomers to Orkney, affectionately known as "ferryloupers" because they arrive in the islands by the ferry, carefully consider which way they first enter Kirkwall, as this will mark them forever as being either an Uppie or a Doonie. This also applies to those who arrive by air. Devious diversions are taken by all concerned to ensure that they enter town through the territory of their team of choice.

Street football has been played in Scotland for hundreds of years. Scone, where the Kings of ancient Scotland were crowned, had its game played on

Shrove Tuesday until 1785. Banffshire had a game, noted as being played in 1629. Church records from Elgin recount the banning of football being played through the town. When Ann and I were guests of the Lothian Family at Ferniehurst Castle near Jedburgh a few years ago, we heard the story of the origin of the Jedburgh "Fasternse'en" Ba' game: commemorating a defence of the castle from English attack when prisoners were decapitated and their heads used as footballs.

A lot of Orcadian heads were knocked about a bit during the 2005 New Year Men's Game. After two hours, the Ba' and the pack were still struggling furiously for supremacy in Broad Street, a few yards away from the Market Cross where the game had begun. The scrum was enveloped in a pall of steam from the heat of the mass of fighting bodies. Just before 2pm, it appeared that the Ba' had been "lost". One observer guessed that it had been smuggled out of the pack to the town library and everybody set off in pursuit, scattering the crowds of spectators in the process. The Ba' was found and the scrum wedged together again, striving for control.

After a further hour, with the Uppie goal in sight, deadlock was broken when the Ba' was thrown to a spectator standing on a nearby roof who hurled it back the way it had come. In spite of this, the Uppies grouped again for a final push. In darkness, four and a half hours after the Ba' had been thrown up at the Cross, the Uppies achieved their fourteenth victory in a row; the longest consecutive period of Uppie New Year Ba' and Christmas Day Game wins since the end of the last war. The Ba' was awarded to Gary Coltherd, who was then raised shoulder-high in triumph by his team-mates as he kissed his hard-won prize.

The 2005 Boys' Christmas Day Game, played on a snow-filled, freezing day, was a classic of its kind. Nearly two and a half hours after the "throw-up of the Ba'", and a few minutes before the start of the Men's Game, the youngsters were still struggling in Broad Street. At one stage, the pack was deluged in a huge fall of snow, sliding off an adjacent roof. With the Ba' and the players jammed into a tight corner, taking a breather whilst still trying to control the Ba', a snowball fight began in the middle of the pack. The Uppies, at one stage within sight of their goal, were gradually forced back and shortly after 4pm, the Doonies had the Ba' in the Harbour when young Jon Tait was awarded the Ba'.

I asked Gary Gibson, a former player and member of the Ba' Committee, how the Ba' winner is chosen. "The victors award the Ba' to one of their team, chosen not just for his performance on the day, but also for his performance over the years that he has been playing the game. There is always some who never get a Ba' and are disappointed, but we all play for the side until the game is over. It's a tremendous feeling, getting a Ba'."

Gary explained that four games were held each year, two on Christmas Day and two on New Year's Day. There is a Boys' Game in the morning, starting at 10.30am, followed by a Men's Game in the afternoon. Gary has won both a Boys' and a Men's Ba' – in 1949, when he was fourteen years old and in later life, in 1967. A further unique distinction is that on the day Gary won his Boys' Ba', his father, Edgar, won the Men's Ba'.

There used to be a Youth's Game as well, between 1897 and 1910, but spectators caused insurmountable problems. The Youth's Game was played after the Boys' Game and before the Men's Game and the temptation to lend a hand, or rather a shoulder, in support of your team was irresistible. Games ended in heated disputes between the players and spectators who had been drawn into the struggle; not only men intervened, but women also were just as likely to become involved. And with three games on the same day, Kirkwall was in chaos.

So how do you tell the difference between an Uppie and a Doonie? Gary was asked this question by a reporter from a women's magazine. "Well," he replied, "all the Uppies are tall, good-looking, Nordic types and all the Doonies are sort of Neanderthal, squat, ugly guys with low foreheads." Gary is an Uppie and his comments appeared in print, much to everyone's amusement. Gary continued, "The truth is that you tell them apart by knowing them, by playing against them since you were a boy. You grow up knowing who is on what side. You also recognise them as descendants of older people that you know."

Gary told me: "Immediately after the end of the game, everyone visits the home of the winner to celebrate. During the course of the evening, they disperse and go and get washed and cleaned up and then come back again. They often carry in a drink or so to help out the host family and the celebration goes on for, well, two or three days, certainly." The Kirkwall Ba' Game is entrenched in the history and culture of the community. The Game is a great leveller, when everybody – policeman, lawyer, doctor, farmer, fisherman, joiner, plumber or builder – meets and competes together in furious and friendly rivalry. As Jim Cromarty told me, "The Game will never die."

I am indebted to John D.M. Robertson, CBE, for information concerning the history and culture of the Kirkwall Ba' Game. His recently published study of the tradition, The Kirkwall Ba', Between the Water and the Wall, has been revised and expanded from his earlier work, Uppies and Doonies, and is required reading for all with an interest in riotous behaviour.

3.
Moray Drive

"When shall we three meet again? In thunder, lightning or in rain?" On a warm September morning the opening lines of Shakespeare's play *Macbeth* came to mind as I sped along the A96 road between Forres and Elgin. The moor here is where the Bard of Avon's three witches foresaw the fate of Macbeth, whilst Bothgowan, near Elgin, is where Macbeth foully murdered and usurped King Duncan of Scotland in 1039.

Elgin was to be the start of my journey, exploring the towns of Moray and the Banffshire villages that cling to the rocky coastline between Elgin and Portsoy. I would then follow the "Malt Whisky Trail" through the "Friendly Town" of Keith to Dufftown, "The Malt Whisky Capital of the World", and return to Elgin by the banks of the River Spey.

Elgin is a well-ordered, attractive town, dominated by the ruins of its cathedral on the banks of the River Lossie. Founded in 1224, the cathedral was so renowned that it became known throughout Europe as "The Lantern of the North", a lantern extinguished 200 years later by rapacious Alisdair Mor mac an Righ, the Wolf of Badenoch; Alisdair burned the cathedral and the town after he was excommunicated by the Bishop of Moray.

As I wandered the well-manicured lawns, I found the last resting place of another, more recent "wolf": Patrick Sellar, the infamous agent of the Countess Duchess of Sutherland, who played a major role in the brutal nineteenth-century evictions of thousands of Highlanders, driven from their homes in Strathnaver to make way for sheep. Sellar was born in Elgin and he and his wife are buried near the boundary wall at the north-east corner of the cathedral.

On the opposite bank are the premises of Johnstons of Elgin, one of the world's most excellent specialists in the manufacture of cashmere. The company was founded more than 200 years ago and their cashmere comes from China and Mongolia, as witnessed by a statue of three goats presented to Johnstons in 1993 by the South Trading Company of China to celebrate more than 140 years of experience of Chinese cashmere. The Mill Shop is a cacophony of colour and wonderful clothes.

I drove north through gentle fields to visit the Palace of Spynie, one of Scotland's most magnificent monuments and founded in 1107. Bishop David Stewart built the great tower of Spynie which is the principal feature of the palace. Spynie is hidden by wonderful woodlands and only the top of the tower can be seen from the road, but a palpable sense of peace and serenity surrounds you the moment you step within its walls.

A few miles from Spynie, near to the Royal Air Force base at Lossiemouth, I stopped to look at the remains of Duffus Castle. A tractor, trailed by a flock of seagulls, was ploughing a field nearby. Duffus Castle was the seat of the Moravia family who were of Flemish origin and came to England with William the Conqueror in 1066. They gave their name, "Moravia", to this part of Scotland.

The Moray Golf Club at Lossiemouth is a fine links course and as I putted out on the 18th green, I recalled its association with Britain's first Labour Prime Minister, Ramsay MacDonald (1866–1937). He was born in Lossiemouth and played there, but club members were so angered by his outspoken hatred of the slaughter taking place during the First World War that they expelled him. When he became Prime Minister in 1924, a vote to reinstate him failed. When he became Prime Minister again in 1929, the club invited him to rejoin their ranks. MacDonald didn't bother to reply.

The character of the coastline changed as I travelled east through Fochabers to Buckie. Broken cliffs tower over tiny, colourful villages: Gordonsburgh, Portessie, Findochty, Portknockie, Cullen and Portsoy. During the great days of the herring fishings in the nineteenth century, these communities thrived. Today, they are just as busy with holidaymakers who come to enjoy the sea air and the superb beaches that line the coast.

Findochty is perhaps one of the most attractive of these villages. The little harbour is crowded with boats of all descriptions, guarded by a white-painted statue of a seated man looking out to sea. Below the figure is a plaque with an inscription from Psalm 107, "These see the works of the LORD and his wonders in the deep." Starlochy Street, by the harbour, is narrow and winding and bordered by cottages, all of which seem to be painted in different colours – a splendid example of Scottish seaside domestic architecture.

Half an hour later, I drove down the steep hill into Cullen. Fading sunlight shadowed the dramatic pinnacles of the "Three Kings" sea stacks near the harbour. I was looking forward to dinner in Portsoy, the next village on my route and where I was to spend the night. There was no doubt what my first course would be: Cullen Skink, a traditional dish originating from Cullen and one of my favourites. "Skink" is the old Scottish name for soup and the main ingredient is haddock, complemented with finely chopped onion, chopped celery, potatoes, vegetable stock, milk and parsley, and perhaps a tablespoonful or three of double cream.

The Station Hotel in Portsoy is a friendly establishment and the proprietors, Euan and Susan Cameron, made my visit memorable; not only because of their welcome, but also because of the quality of the food they provided and believe me, the Cullen Skink was everything that I had hoped it would be. The following morning I explored the harbour, known for its annual Traditional Small Boat Festival (8–9 July), an event that attracts 20,000 visitors to the town and celebrates the maritime and cultural heritage of the north east of Scotland.

The next morning, I headed south west down the A95 towards Keith and the heartland of Scotland's famous single-malt whiskies. The landscape changed again, from the rugged grandeur of the coast to the fertile farmlands that grow the high-quality, golden barley used in the production of whisky. The Strathisla Distillery in Keith is the oldest in Scotland and has been in business since 1786. I pondered these matters as I stood on the Auld Brig that crosses the River Isla in the centre of Keith, built in 1609 and the oldest such structure in Scotland. Thomas and Janet Murray built the bridge after their son drowned there fording the river.

I arrived in Dufftown and fortuitously parked outside the Whisky Shop. Everything you ever wanted to know about *uisge beatha*, the Water of Life, will be found there and in the local Whisky Museum. The town sits at the confluence of the Dullan Burn and the River Fiddich, a major tributary of the River Spey. The Glenfiddich Distillery, opened on Christmas Day 1887 by its founder, William Grant, invites you to tour the distillery and sample their product.

Nearby is Balvanie Castle, a graceful thirteenth-century ruin that gives its name to another of Scotland's most outstanding malts, The Balvenie. Visitors are welcome at seven more distilleries in the immediate vicinity of Dufftown, at Pittyvaich, Dufftown, Benrinnes, Glenallachie, Mortlach, Glendullan and Convalmore.

Most of the barrels used by the industry come from the Speyside Cooperage, a few miles north from Dufftown. I stopped to have a word with Adeline Murphy, the Visitor Centre Manager. The cooperage makes and repairs 100,000 casks each year and they dominate the view. Some, positioned throughout the splendid gardens, are used as picnic shelters.

The principal river of Morayshire is the mighty Spey, the UK's fastest flowing stream. As well as being central to the production of malt whisky, the Spey is one of Europe's most famous salmon rivers and as an angler, I fell in love with it more years ago than I care to remember. Whisky and fishing are inextricably linked, so it was appropriate to visit Craigellachie and the home of my favourite whisky, The Macallan, often described as being the "Rolls Royce" of single malts.

After paying my respects to the traditional small, hand-beaten copper stills in the distillery, I drove down to the Spey where the company has a salmon beat. Afternoon sunlight sparkled on the crystal-clear stream. A best-bibbed black and white dipper hunted for insects amongst the stones along the margins whilst visiting anglers cast for salmon in the river. In the fishing hut, the talk was all about fishing, assisted by a comfortable dram of The Macallan.

My last call on this journey was in the small town of Rothes to visit the Glen Grant Distillery, one of the first to bottle its whisky as a single malt, rather than using it in blended whisky. The Glen Grant Distillery Gardens are just as impressive as their whisky; old apple trees and rhododendrons planted in the 1880s, ornamental areas filled with plants from America, China and the Himalayas, and a rustic bridge over the Black Burn which flows through the garden on its way to the distillery and the River Spey.

I climbed to the bridge where my guide opened a safe in the cliff face. It was constructed by James Grant, "The Major", in the 1870s so that he could serve his guests with a dram during an after-dinner stroll. The safe contained two bottles of the finest Glen Grant single malt and a cup on a chain so that water from the burn could be added to the straw-coloured liquid.

At the end of my fantastic journey, I drove home, back along the A96, my mind full of the sights and sounds that I had experienced on my travels through Moray and Banffshire; the serenity of the glorious ruins of the Lantern of the North; tumbled towers and quiet courtyards; of endless waves beating on strong harbour walls; colourful cottages clustered by the shore; the cry of wheeling gulls; the pleasure of Cullen Skink; the splash of a silver Spey salmon, and the warmth and pleasure of a golden glass of the Water of Life.

4.
Ballindalloch Castle

Ballindalloch Castle, "The Pearl of the North", is a wondrous surprise. The castle can't be seen from the road. Even as you approach along the tree-lined route through immaculately manicured grounds, it hides itself from view until almost the last moment.

I parked my car amidst the russet of an autumn afternoon and walked round a neatly trimmed beech hedge. This was when the beauty of Ballindalloch was exposed: calm, serene, turreted and towered, with crenellated gables that seemed to float above its pearl-grey walls.

Before me lay a lawn that dreams are made of, busy with black and white pied-wagtails. The sound of collared doves echoed from the woods. Trees that were old when I was a boy stood guard over the ancient home of the Macpherson-Grant families. Beyond the lawn, well-tended fields swept down to the banks of the swiftly flowing River Spey.

Scotland is resplendent with castles, most of which are grim reminders of the country's turbulent past. Hardly a square yard of my native land is untouched by signs of its violent birth and vigorous adolescence.

The ordered discipline of Ballindalloch belies this truth, although it has had its share of turmoil; during the religious wars of the 1640s, James Graham, Marquis of Montrose (1612–1650), knocked the castle about a bit. But Clan Grant, through their astuteness, weathered most of the storms that buffeted the Highlands.

This astuteness is as much in evidence today as it was in times past. The present Laird, Lady Clare Macpherson-Grant, and her husband, Oliver Russell, have lived at Ballindalloch for the past twenty-five years and their care for and love of this precious inheritance is self-evident.

Lady Clare was a Deputy Lieutenant for Banffshire from 1991 until 1998, when she was appointed Vice Lord-Lieutenant. In 2002, the Queen appointed her as Lord-Lieutenant for Banffshire. Oliver Russell is a former Page of Honour to Her Majesty and a member of the Queen's Bodyguard for Scotland, the Royal Company of Archers.

Lady Clare is a handsome woman with a wonderful smile. She said: "We have been continuing the renovations that my parents started in 1967. They took down the most recent wing which had been added in 1878. The family called it the carbuncle because it spoiled the entire castle.

"I was brought up here and educated by a Wee Free governess. I had seen my mother run the estate and when I took over, it had much the same staff. It's been a great challenge and it has been wonderful to have done the things that we have done together and survived.

"We try to refurbish a room every year. When I was five, there was one bathroom in the house and if it rained, we ran around with buckets. My parents did a lot to restore the property, including the installation of eight bathrooms. When we came back we did a lot, too, including more bathrooms. If one generation doesn't do any renovation, it nearly brings it all down."

The Grant ancestors came to Britain from Normandy with William the Conqueror (1066) and in the fifteenth century, King James IV (1488–1513) gave the lands of Ballindalloch to Patrick Grant. Different branches of Clan Grant have held the estate ever since. The original structure – the corner tower of the present building – built in 1546, took the form a Z-plan castle.

"We had to completely commercialise the whole estate when we returned because there was no income coming in," Lady Clare said. "We started opening the house to the public about eleven years ago and now have fifty people staying in our estate houses from March to October, fishing, shooting and playing golf on our new golf course."

Lady Clare's husband, Oliver, said: "We want to preserve the castle but not to preserve it in aspic. Some old castles are like museums and one tries to avoid that here. This is a family home and things have to work. When it comes to renovation, you must look 100 years ahead. I can be fairly sure that the things I have done here will still be around in 100 years time.

"They may not reflect me, or my personality, but they will still be here. It's a balance between the commercial aspects of the estate and its role as a home. The income comes from farming, forestry, shooting, fishing and tourism. Clare's great-grandfather started the Aberdeen-Angus breed [of cattle] and we still farm them today."

The Ballindalloch herd of Aberdeen-Angus is the oldest herd in the world, the result of the vision of three men: Hugh Watson of Keillor in Angus (1780–1865), William McCombie of Tillyfour in Aberdeenshire (1805–1880), and Sir George Macpherson-Grant, 2nd Bart of Ballindalloch, who inherited the estate in 1850 at the age of twenty-one years.

The herd is descended from Aberdeenshire's traditional black cattle, known locally as "doddies" and "hummlies", and the breed is now famous throughout the world. Sir George was determined to establish the Ballindalloch herd as the finest of the breed and this tradition continues under the guidance of the Macpherson-Grants and their stockman, Ian Spence.

The best-known breeder of Aberdeen-Angus cattle was the late Queen Mother. Her association with the breed began during her early years at Glamis Castle and she was Patron of the Aberdeen-Angus Cattle Society for sixty-five years until her death in 2002.

The Queen Mum, as she was affectionately known, established her own herd at the Castle of Mey in Caithness in 1964. Castle of Mey and Ballindalloch have always worked together to continue to improve the breed and the Queen Mother was a frequent visitor at Ballindalloch.

The Queen Mother was also Patron of Queen Mary's Clothing Guild, one of her favourite charities founded in 1882, and Clare Macpherson-Grant Russell has been Scottish chairman of the Guild since 1986.

The Guild is a nationwide network of women who knit with wool donated to them by supporters of the charity. Each year, Ballindalloch Castle is the gathering centre for the items completed in Scotland and for those who did the knitting. The Queen Mother invariably attended this happy occasion and, no doubt, also took the opportunity to have a shrewd look at the Aberdeen-Angus herd when she was there.

I turned from the splendid lawn and entered the castle. Almost immediately, I was aware of being in a family home, rather than a castle. Nothing seemed to be on display, but everywhere you looked there was something of interest, some beautiful object, piece of furniture or portrait to catch the eye: eighteenth-century pistols over the fireplace, a Sheraton corner cupboard and Chinese Chippendale-style chairs.

This "lived in" look pervades the whole house; the library, with its amazing collection of more than 25,000 books, collected mainly by Colonel William Grant in the early eighteenth century and by Sir John Macpherson-Grant; Lady Macpherson-Grant's room, with its wonderful four-poster bed made in cherry wood in 1860.

Family portraits adorn the walls, including one of General James Grant (1720–1806), who in 1770 built the part of the house that contains the present-day drawing room. Grant was born at Ballindalloch but spent most of his life fighting Britain's wars around the world.

Grant took part in the Battle of Fontenoy in Flanders in May 1745 and was back in Scotland in April 1746 to join in the rout of Bonnie Prince Charlie's rebel force at Culloden. He fought against the French and the Cherokee Indians and was briefly Governor of Florida (1763).

Most famously, when illness forced him to return to England in 1771, on the brink of the American War of Independence, he declared in parliament that he could "march from one end of the continent to the other with five thousand men". He learned different at Bunkers Hill, Trenton, Boston, New York and other engagements.

The General was famous for his love of fine food and drink. As I stood in the dining room, the largest room in the castle and formerly the Great Hall, I swear I heard him calling for a toast to His Majesty. A portrait of King George III, painted by Allan Ramsay, was presented to Grant in recognition of his military service in America and it hangs in the dining room.

Lady Clare said of her illustrious ancestor, "He died the fattest man in Great Britain and still wanders along the passage handing out drams."

Ballindalloch is well-endowed with ghosts. A bedroom in the Pink Tower, the oldest part of the castle, holds the spirit of an unknown woman, seen sitting in a chair, wearing a pink crinoline gown and a large straw hat. The ghost of the General, mounted on a white horse, is said to ride the estate boundaries every night. The ghost of a daughter of the castle, jilted in love, has been seen crossing the bridge over the River Avon to post a letter to her errant lover.

Another love is to be found at Ballindalloch, in Lady Clare's latest book, *I Love Food*. The book is, like the house, as much a celebration of family as it is about her love of cooking. "We wanted it to be a bit different. There are favourite recipes, family photographs, prayers, poems and paintings, as well as information about the castle. And it's the only recipe book around with a section on food for dogs!" she said.

I left the house and stepped out into the warm evening. The pied-wagtails still played on the lawn and doves still called from the woods. Lengthening shadows touched the old castle, sending shafts of sunlight dancing amidst its towers and turrets. It was hard to leave. My enduring memory of Ballindalloch is of a wonderful, happy, family home.

Ballindalloch Castle lies twelve miles to the north of Grantown-on-Spey on the A95 Grantown to Craigellachie road at Bridge of Avon. For further information, contact: The Estate Office, Ballindalloch Castle, Banffshire, Scotland AB37 9AX; Tel: 01807 500 205; Fax: 01807 500 210; Website: http://www.ballindalloch castle.co.uk; Email: enquiries@ballindallochcastle.co.uk

5.
Helmsdale

I stood at the end of the pier at Helmsdale Harbour. A silver-grey sea merged into the cloud-darkened sky. The breakwater of the old harbour wall was clustered with the black, statuesque shapes of cormorants, crowded together like semi-quavers on a page of music. Arctic tern wheeled overhead. A group of white-cloaked eider ducks probed for food in the shallows. The deep throb of the engine of a returning fishing boat filled the air.

The opposite wall, at the entrance to the harbour, sparkled with light reflected from a huge, sculptured fish-like shape, part whale and part salmon; a work commissioned by Timespan, the Helmsdale heritage organisation, from the artist Julian Meredith. It is constructed out of a series of stainless steel, triangular-shaped pieces, each piece being of a different size. It celebrates the whales that are often seen from the harbour and the salmon that return through the harbour to their natal home in the Helmsdale River.

Behind me lay the little village, clinging to the sides of the yellow-bright, gorse-covered hills that guard the village and the mouth of the Helmsdale River; one of Scotland's most famous salmon streams, much loved by HRH Prince Charles and countless numbers of other anglers who come to the far north from all over the world to fish in its peat-stained waters for *Salmo salar*, the King of Fish.

The story of Helmsdale is inextricably linked to the sea and to fishing. People have lived and worked here for thousands of years. The village has weathered the less-than-friendly visitations of Viking invaders, endless clan squabbles and the depredations of the dreadful days of the Highland Clearances during the nineteenth century when Kildonan Strath was cleared of people to make way for more profitable sheep.

Some of the dispossessed were allotted small plots of land at Gartymore, to the south of Helmsdale, where they were expected to set up home and support their families. These harsh beginnings gave birth to the Land League, through which the crofters fought a long and acrimonious battle with their landlords and with the government for security of tenure of their properties. Eventually, in 1886, this was won by the passing of the first Crofting Act.

I got lost once in Helmsdale, which is difficult to do because the village has few streets. But it was a happy accident. Until then, I had passed through, either travelling south from our home in Caithness or hurrying north again with never enough time to stand and stare. Since then, I often visit Helmsdale to explore its history and walk its well-ordered streets. The village was laid out by the Duke of Sutherland to accommodate those cleared from his lands, a fact commemorated in the street names he chose for his new town.

The streets parallel to the river were named after the Duke's Sutherland holdings: Sutherland Street (the family owned most of the county in those days) and Dunrobin Street (in honour of his fairytale castle to the north of Golspie). The streets running in the opposite direction were named after his lands in England: Stafford Street and Stittenham Road. Before the clearances, Helmsdale and its hinterland areas had 2,000 people. Today, it is home to about 600.

I had come that morning to speak to some of the people who call Helmsdale home, and to ask them about the life and history of their village, and my first call was on Adam Macpherson at his general store in Dunrobin Street. Adam was born in Helmsdale. His grandfather started the business and his father followed in his father's footsteps. Adam himself has been there for the past twenty-five years. He told me, "I love staying here. I think that it is a very beautiful little village. I won't be moving. No, I'll be here forever. I was born just next door to the shop."

In the nineteenth century, Helmsdale was one of the most important herring fishing stations on the north-east coast. During the short summer season, more than 200 boats crowded the harbour, setting out to sea each day in search of the "silver darlings". The village bustled with the activity of cleaning and curing the herring, which were salted and packed into barrels and exported to the Baltic and Europe. Such was the efficiency of the operation that fish caught in July could be on the table in Europe by early September.

The advent of the Great War and the Russian Revolution brought these glory days to an end and by the 1960s, the fleet had turned to fishing for white fish, cod and haddock. When stocks of these fish began to decline, Helmsdale's importance as a fishing port declined with them. Today, the few boats left primarily fish for prawns, lobsters and crab, which provide a good living because they are under less pressure than white fish stocks. Alex Jappy is the Harbour Master and I met him in the nineteenth-century Red Herring House, a herring curing yard built by the Duke of Sutherland, which now serves as the Harbour Master's office.

I asked Alex what he saw as the future for Helmsdale Harbour and his answer was unequivocal: yachts. Until not so long ago, fewer than eight or nine yachts visited the harbour each year. Now, the number has risen to over ninety. Most are visitors from England, sailing up the west coast of Scotland and through the Caledonian Canal to Inverness. From there, it is a day's sail to Helmsdale. This makes Helmsdale the ideal place to rest before an onward journey to Wick, thence across the broken waters of the Pentland Firth to the Orkney Islands.

Alex told me that additional pontoons were being installed to meet the growing demand and that this increase in visitors was bringing new life to the community. "To start with, most of the boats just stopped overnight. Now, some are staying for a week, hiring a car to explore the area, enjoying its culture and history, and enjoying the fresh sea food and local produce available in our restaurants and pubs. For centuries, Scotland's most notable export was its people, now, it seems to me, the position is reversed as more and more people from the south recognise the quality of the life that we have and want to share it," he said.

The confidence Alex Jappy has in the future of Helmsdale is nowhere better reflected than in Timespan. This award-winning heritage centre has become a focal point for the community. Indeed, it owes its existence to the determination of the community to record its history and commemorate those who helped to shape it. At the wheel of this enthusiastic juggernaut is Timespan Director, Rachel Skeen, who steers the ever-expanding interests of Timespan with consummate skill, supported by an equally enthusiastic staff and a hard-working board of directors and volunteers.

Timespan has just completed work on a "geology garden", overlooking the river. The garden is peopled with huge rocks from virtually every period of geological time, each stone accompanied by a brief description of its place in the making and formation of the north of Scotland. The Timespan gallery, the only public art gallery in Sutherland, hosts exhibitions and workshops from visiting artists from around the world – this year, artists from Finland and Canada, as well as from Scotland. Alex Jappy is helping with the restoration of a Fifie, a design of fishing boat that was in use in Helmsdale from the 1850s until well into the twentieth century.

However, the key function of Timespan is to record and display records and artefacts that illuminate the life and times of Helmsdale, and it does this with unparalleled success, attracting thousands of visitors each year. Timespan has also introduced the UK's first ever GPS (Global Positioning System) visitor experience, which leads visitors round the site of Scotland's only Gold Rush. The Gold Rush began in 1869 when Robert Gilchrist returned to his native village from prospecting in Australia. Gilchrist found gold in Kildonan Burn at Baile an Or and shortly thereafter, 300 men had arrived at the site to seek their fortune. Gold may still be found in the Kildonan Burn today and visitors can try their luck panning for it.

One of Helmsdale's most famous recent residents was the novelist Barbara Cartland, author of 723 books. Barbara Cartland married into the McCorquodale family who lived at Kilphedir and fished the river. She was famous also for her love of pink chiffon clothing and jewellery. One of her great friends, the late Nancy Sinclair, shared this love. Nancy, a happy, welcoming woman, was a Helmsdale institution and lived surrounded by an astonishing array of mementos and artefacts, not the least of which is a life-sized figure of Marilyn Monroe, skirt blowing, in a bathroom, and a similar-sized one of Elvis Presley in the sitting room.

Rather than setting off to a fashion career in Paris, Nancy came north to help her mother run the Navidale House Hotel to the north of Helmsdale. I asked what she thought of her decision now: "All I could think was that there was nothing here but sheep!" In time, Nancy opened La Mirage restaurant in Dunrobin Street, which became one of the north's most notable places to dine. Decorated entirely in her favourite pink style, La Mirage was featured in press and on television and attracted a clientele that included household names from stage and screen. Last year, Nancy was appointed Chieftain of the Helmsdale Highland Games.

Back at the harbour, I called at an Aladdin's Cave of a shop in one of Helmsdale's oldest buildings in Helmsdale to meet the owner, Lorna Sangster, an ebullient woman with a sparkling smile and a deep love of her adopted home. Lorna was born in Edinburgh but has lived in Helmsdale for many years. The shop hosts an amazing display of local and worldwide craft items, including the famous Helmsdale Pottery made by David and Penny Woodley.

The building dates from 1745, when it housed government troops billeted there after Bonnie Prince Charlie's sad uprising. The lower part was used as stables for the soldiers' horses; the narrow slits that ventilated the stables have been uncovered. The upper floor was living quarters, whilst the officer in charge lived in the house next door. Later, the building was used as a granary; tenants paid their rent to the laird in money and in produce.

In the aftermath of the Clearances, when people where starving throughout the Highlands, the grain that they grew for their laird was shipped south. A statue of a family – father, mother and child – has been erected on the hill overlooking the harbour to commemorate these times and the suffering of the people who were evicted. The family is looking out to sea, which so many were destined to sail, to Canada, Australia, New Zealand and South Africa. Today, their descendants return to search the straths of Sutherland for lost stories of their loved ones, and to pay their respects to the land and people that gave them birth.

As I turned from the harbour, the day had ended. The sea glistened steely blue and I drove home thinking of Alex Jappy's parting words when I asked him what was special about Helmsdale: "The people, really, they are always kind and friendly. That is what makes Helmsdale such a special place, the people." Amen to that, I thought.

6.
Assynt Revisited

Alastair MacAskill is a big man with a big personality. His soft voice resonates with love for his Assynt homeland and he is Chairman of the Assynt Foundation, a community group that now owns 44,000 acres of land in the area. I met Alastair at Glencanisp Lodge near Lochinver and asked him how the 450 families in this remote corner of North West Sutherland managed to acquire Glencanisp and Drumrunie, two of Scotland's most magnificent estates.

Alastair told me, "I had heard on the grape vine that the estates were coming up for sale and a short time later my friend Bill Ritchie put to me the idea that the community should bid for them. I was not sure. However, he suggested that it was possible that they would fall into the hands of owners who might be less than conscious of their responsibility to the community and that the only way to avoid this happening was for the community itself to buy the land."

Bill Ritchie had been one of the leaders of the historic crofter-led £300,000 buy out of the 21,300-acre North Assynt Estate in 1993. The estate had been placed on the market when the company that owned it went into liquidation. It was proposed that it should be broken up into seven lots – showing little regard for the impact that this would have had on the crofting families who lived and worked there, as their forefathers had done for generations before them.

Within a short space of time, the crofters had prepared a bid to buy the estate and reports began to appear in the press about this 'audacious attempt by a few crofters in the North West Highlands' to win back the land taken from their ancestors during the terrible years of the nineteenth-century

Highland Clearances. The crofters' campaign caught the public's imagination and six months after the decision to launch the bid, the newly-formed Assynt Crofters Trust took back their land.

Thus, when Glencanisp and Drumrunie came on the market, there was an in-built support mechanism for a local buy out. At a meeting in Lochinver in February 2005 the community voted by a margin of two to one in favour of bidding for Glencanisp and Drumrunie; the estates had been run in the past as sporting "playgrounds", with an abundance of game and very few people. Now, however, the local community would have to raise nearly £3 million to complete the purchase. They did but it was a close-run thing.

Under land reform law introduced by the Scottish Parliament, a community wishing to buy their land has six months in which to do so, starting from the date that it first announces its intention to submit an offer. The Scottish Executive Land Fund, set up to help land purchase, and the Community Land Fund, a similar fund operated by Highlands and Islands Enterprise, pledged £2 million towards the cost of the purchase, but for the people that Alistair led, time would run out on 3 June.

With six weeks left to go, the community was still short of £900,000 pounds and it was beginning to look very much as though their famous bid was heading for failure. At that time, Alastair MacAskill commented, "No one is giving up hope but we don't have long, and unless we have a clear idea of where the money is coming from, we couldn't even ask the owners for an extension on the time we have to buy their estates."

But help was at hand. In May, at the instigation of the John Muir Trust, named after Scotland's most famous conservationist, the England-based Tubney Trust came forward with a surprise donation of £550,000. When the news was announced, Alistair said, "We are going to do it. We are highly optimistic that we will get the necessary funds by the deadline. Three weeks ago we were short of £900,000. Since then we have raised £700,000. Not bad for such a small community. We are hopeful that some of the other funding bodies will now help to close the gap." They did.

I asked Alastair how he had felt when it was signed, sealed and delivered.

He smiled and touched his head, "Do you not see all these grey hairs? But I will tell you how I felt. Yes, we were elated, but it was tempered with the realisation of the enormity of the task that we were undertaking. I think that it was the writer John Galsworthy who said, 'Idealism can be directly measured in proportion to a person's distance from the problem.' We are at no distance at all from the problem. This is our home and we went into this with our eyes wide open."

My first visit to Assynt and Drumrunie, many years ago, opened my eyes. Our children were at school at the time and the school had arranged an adventure weekend at Elphin, near Drumrunie. A woman was required to "chaperon" the girls in the group and since our daughter was in the party, my wife, Ann, agreed to go along. I accompanied them in my capacity as an angler, to introduce some of the children to the joys of fishing for wild brown trout. We arrived after dark and the next morning I went outside to see what I could see.

When I was confronted with the vastness of the landscape, my heart missed a beat. It was as though I had stepped into a paradise of mountains and moorland. Dramatic, uncompromising peaks crowded the view: Cul Mor (849m); Cul Beg (789m); the long, grey shoulder of Canisp (846m); and Suilven (731m), the "Pillar Mountain" of the Vikings. They were etched into a clear, cloudless sky, almost as if I could reach out my hand and touch them. Mirror-calm lochs, stippled with rising trout, reflected their image; the long, silver-blue ribbon of Veyatie, crooked Cam Loch and, at the centre of the Inverpolly Nature Reserve, magnificent Sionascaig, winding around a jagged shoreline for a distance of more than seventeen miles.

Later that morning, I tramped a track on the north shore of the Cam Loch with a few of the boys, trout rods at the ready. After a mile or so, we climbed north west into the hills to find two lochs where I knew that catching trout was virtually guaranteed: little Loch a'Chroisg and finger-like Lochan Fada. With Canisp to our right and the enormous, intimidating bulk of Suilven ahead, we spent a happy few hours and caught enough trout to provide breakfast for the whole party the following morning.

I have been returning to Assynt and Drumrunie ever since and every time I do so, I still experience that sudden shock of pleasure as I descend from Glen Oykle and catch the first glimpse of this splendid wonderland. One of my heroes, who had a life-long love affair with Assynt, is the late Norman MacCaig, awarded the Queen's Gold Medal for Poetry in 1986. My great regret is that I never called to see him because we had a lot in common. Like me, he was born in Edinburgh, went to the same school that I attended, The Royal High, and, again like me, he loved hill loch fishing for wild brown trout.

You will find copies of his books at Scotland's most remote bookshop, Achins, at Inverkirkaig, where the River Kirkaig tumbles into Enard Bay. MacCaig's works are constant best sellers at Achins. Here is one of my favourite's poems:

On the North Side of Suilven

The three-inch-wide streamlet
trickles over its own fingers
down the sandstone slabs
of my favourite mountain.

Like the Amazon it'll reach the sea
Like the Volga
it'll forget its own language.

Its water goes down my throat
With glassy coldness,
Like something suddenly remembered.

I drink
Its freezing vocabulary
And half understand the purity
Of all beginnings.

The broken bounds of Assynt and Drumrunie instil in all who know them a deep love for this amazing landscape. Few express this love more eloquently and passionately than Allan MacRae, the present chairman of the Assynt Crofters Trust. His determination to enhance and preserve the crofting way of life is self-evident, from the moment he begins to recall how the Trust has survived and expanded since that momentous day in 1993 when they bought back their land. Allan encapsulated this for me when I met him recently. He told me, "Without our land, we are nothing."

Allan's Crofters Trust supports the aspirations of "new boys" in town, the Assynt Foundation, of which more than 25% of the community are now members. Derek Louden is the Foundation development manager and he, too, is passionately committed to the aims of the Foundation: to create opportunities for local people to live and work on the land; encourage and support the entrepreneurial ambitions of local people; get people back on the land by creating crofts and smallholdings; create employment; safeguard and enhance the natural heritage and landscape on behalf of the nation.

You, too, can help the Foundation achieve these objectives by joining "Friends of Assynt Foundation". As such, you will receive regular newsletters and progress reports. The Foundation is based at Glencanisp Lodge, a traditional Highland sporting lodge set amidst ancient woodlands overlooking little island-dotted Loch Druim Suardalain. Eventually, the Foundation hopes to let out Glencanisp Lodge to visitors, as they intended to do with other properties that they now own. I can think of no finer place in all of Scotland in which to spend precious time.

The face of land tenure in Scotland was radically altered by the primary actions of the Assynt Crofters Trust and this, in my opinion, encouraged other Scottish communities to follow suit – including the bold, spectacular decision of the Assynt Foundation to bid for and win the ownership of Glencanisp and Drumrunie for the local community. Before I left the lodge, Alastair MacAskill told me, "We do not view ourselves as landowners – we see ourselves as custodians of the land." As I drove home through the mountains, I knew that I had left Assynt in safe hands.

7.

Durness

Not so many years ago, a few days before Easter, a crofter was herding half a dozen donkeys along the narrow road from Rhiconich to Durness in North West Sutherland. In the process, he collected behind him a convoy of motorists who were angry about being unable to get past.

Eventually, the crofter left his donkeys and walked back to the leading vehicle. The agitated driver wound down his window but before he could utter a single word, the recalcitrant crofter politely asked, "Excuse me, Sir, can you tell me, is this the way to Jerusalem?"

It is this wry, laconic sense of humour that marks out the Highlander from the Lowland Scot and it is a characteristic I have always admired. The story is true and I first heard it during one of my early visits to this most glorious and dramatic part of the land that I love and call home.

I am an angler and hill walker, and was first drawn to Durness by the lure of its famous wild brown trout lochs and salmon and sea-trout fishing on the River Dionard and in the Kyle of Durness – and by the urge to explore the ragged ridge of Foinaven (914m), grey-shouldered Arkle (787m), green Cranstackie (801m) and the wilderness hills of Cape Wrath.

The township of Durness clings to the edge of the sea-bird-clad cliffs that protect this remote community from Atlantic storms. People have lived here for thousands of years, from the Mesolithic hunter-gatherers who arrived at the end of the last Ice Age some 8,000 years ago, to the Neolithic men who followed them and, subsequently, their Pictish descendants.

Warrior Vikings invaded in the later years of the ninth century and ruled the Highlands and Islands for more than 500 years. During this time, this part of Sutherland became home to Clan Mackay: "The first Lord of

Reay was a Mackay and he and his relations owned all of the land that extended from the western seaboard, between Assynt and Cape Wrath, to the Caithness frontier in the east. He was described as the leader of four thousand fighting men."

On a spring morning last April, I set out for Durness from my home in Tongue to speak to a less-warlike member of the clan, Iris Mackay. My intention was to try to discover what it was that had made, and still makes, Durness (population 350) one of the most vibrant communities in Scotland. Iris is an immediately striking personality, with a wonderful smile and a wonderfully soft, Highland voice. A black Labrador dog, tail-wagging, also greeted me and we relaxed in Iris's sitting room chatting over home-baked scones and shortbread.

Iris Mackay owns a treasure trove of a shop, Mather's Mini Market, close to her house on the main A838 Tongue to Durness road. The shop overlooks the golden sands and blue seas of Sango Bay and has been a family business for 100 years. Iris is still known as Iris Mather although she has been married to her husband, Donnie, for more than thirty-eight years.

I asked Iris what made Durness special for her and she paused whilst considering her reply: "It is the community spirit and the life style that we have here. People are important. Everybody is equal. I grew up here and could never survive in a town or city. Of course, over the years, things change, attitudes change, but there is still the same sense of communal responsibility for where we live, and for the way in which we live."

One of the best-attended events in North Sutherland is the Durness Highland Gathering, held on the last Friday in July. Iris has been a member of the Gathering committee for more than three decades and has been chairperson for fourteen years. The competitions – from tossing the caber to highland dancing – are free of charge and open to everyone, no matter from which country they come, and in the evening there is a Highland Gathering dance in the village hall, which always attracts an enthusiastic full house.

Iris Mackay also plays an active role in the Durness Community Council, which has an affiliated charitable organisation, the Durness

Development Group. The Group has promoted a wide range of activities to sustain the community and to provide employment and tourist opportunities for locals and visitors alike.

Their work has had an enormous impact, particularly through the establishment of the "Cape Wrath Challenges". The week includes what is generally regarded to be the toughest marathon in the UK – forty-two kilometres with a climb of over 736 metres, beginning at the east side of the Kyle of Durness, out to Cape Wrath Lighthouse and then back again. The event takes place in May and attracts more than 200 runners.

There are other, less taxing runs during the festival: a half marathon, the Sangmore and Loch Meadaidh hill run, and a ten kilometre run. But the Cape Wrath Challenges are not only about testing your stamina along some golden strand or heather-bordered track, they are also about people: a wide range of social events are organised, designed to involve every member of the community, their guests and visitors.

On the first evening of the week there is a Meet & Greet wine and cheese event with a welcome talk about the area. This is held in the Village Hall and is free of charge. During the week, there is a general knowledge Quiz Night with teams of local people and visitors in the Sango Sands Oasis pub, as well as abseiling down Smoo Cave – sixty-one metres long, forty metres wide and fifteen metres high, once the haunt of smugglers and brigands. Local wine producers, Balnakeil Wines, arrange wine tasting and there are sheepdog trial demonstrations where top-class dogs work with their shepherds.

There is also time to brush up on your Scottish Country Dancing skills, accompanied by local musicians and expert dancers. "Square Wheels" offer mountain biking and instruction for exploring the peat tracks around Durness, and there is angling on the world-famous Durness limestone lochs, Caladail, Borralie, Croispol and little Lanlish. Visitors can also enjoy a round of golf, where players must drive across the Atlantic, a wide bay dividing the 9th tee from the flagpole that marks the position of the cup on the distant green.

As well as the activities noted above, the local Countryside Ranger organises guided walks to bird-watching sites – puffins galore – and areas renowned for the diversity of their flora and fauna, including wonderful plants such as the unique Scottish primrose, *Primula scotica*. Members of the Durness Archaeology Field Group are also on hand to guide visitors to sites of historical and archaeological interest nearby.

If you need to test your sea legs, then the Cape Wrath Charters Company's vessel, *The Nimrod*, carries up to twelve passengers and offers the chance to see, close-up, some of the most dramatic sea-cliffs to be found anywhere around the British Isles. Finally, the Cape Wrath Challenges week ends on the Saturday evening with a splendid ceilidh, complete with a traditional ceilidh band and a buffet featuring the best of locally produced and prepared food.

In September, Durness bustles again with the annual Sheepdog Trials at Keoldale Farm, overlooking the Kyle of Durness and backed by the mountains of Strath Dionard. The event attracts some of Scotland's finest dog-handlers, thanks to the hard work of the small band of enthusiasts who organise the event and to Keoldale Farm manager, Jock Sutherland, a well-kent face at trials around the country. It is always an early start, from 7am, with business being completed at about 6pm, but entirely enthralling, as much for visitors as it is for those taking part.

As well as the September Sheepdog Trials, a Music & Food Festival is generally arranged and last year this was incorporated into the John Lennon Northern Lights Festival. As a youth, John Lennon, the famous member of the "Fab Four", The Beatles, used to visit Durness on holiday when he stayed with his aunt, Elizabeth Sutherland. This connection is commemorated by a splendid John Lennon garden next to the Village Hall.

The Festival featured some of Scotland and the UK's most prestigious musicians and composers, including Sir Peter Maxwell Davies, Master of the Queen's Music. There were classical, jazz, traditional Scottish music and popular music performances. Theatre and film were also represented, as well as poets and writers. The event was an enormous success and captured the title "Best New Festival" in the UK Festival Awards competition.

However, the heart of any community is its school and, after leaving Iris Mackay at her shop unloading the weekly delivery of supplies, I went in search of Graham Bruce, head teacher at Durness Primary School, where he and his colleague look after nineteen pupils. I found Graham at the School House and asked him what it was that had attracted him to Durness.

"When I was ten years old, we came north on a family holiday and I never forgot the experience, particularly the seemingly unending drive along the north coast from Caithness to get here. It took all day. The road was very narrow, with passing places, and there was no causeway over the Kyle of Tongue then. But I never forgot it and when I saw an advert for a teacher in Durness, I immediately applied. That was twenty-four years ago."

Like Iris Mackay, Graham identified the strong sense of community spirit as being the well-spring of life in this remote corner of Scotland: "It is a good community to live in," he told me. "People pull together and work together in an almost old-fashioned way. If something has to be done, they simply do it and make things happen. They are really nice people."

Graham is chairman of the Durness Development Group and is immensely proud of what the Group has achieved, not the least of which was the communal effort involved in funding the building of the new village hall; in use seven days a week by the local youth club and for badminton, indoor football and bowls, table tennis, country dancing, social events and meetings. The hall has become the key venue for groups throughout North West Sutherland.

I left the school house and drove to the Loch Croispol Bookshop and Restaurant for lunch. No visit to Durness is complete without a visit to the bookshop, run by Kevin Crowe and his partner Simon Long. They serve simple, excellent food in a comforting atmosphere, surrounded by books, where you may browse for as long as you please.

After lunch I visited Balnakeil to watch golfers attempting the "shot across the Atlantic", and wind-surfers and canoeists splashing amongst the green, white-topped waves. Also, to pay my respects to Rob Don (1714–1778), the Gaelic poet, revered in the north and known as the Robert Burns of the Highlands: "I was born in the winter, among the lowering mountains, and my first sight of the world, snow and wind about my ears." He lies at rest here in the old graveyard overlooking the bay.

With the afternoon sun setting, I turned for home. One more stop along the way, near Portnacon, by deep Loch Eriboll, and the remains of an earth-house built and inhabited some 2,000 years ago, now barely visible amongst the bracken and heather that has grown over the roof. I climbed down the broken stairs to the dark inner chamber and listened to the silence. I know that it was just my imagination but I thought that I could faintly hear the voices and laughter of the people who had once lived there – along their road to Jerusalem.

8.
Bagpipe Music

When I served with the East Lowland Divisional District Territorial Army Column, I used to give the commentary for our Pipes & Drums as they Beat Retreat on Edinburgh Castle esplanade. The ceremony of Beating Retreat grew out of the days when troops retreat into a defensive positions at nightfall. It was an honour for our band to be asked to Beat Retreat and it was the principal social event in our year, followed by a drinks party in Edinburgh Castle's Officer's Mess and a magisterial piobaireachd from our Pipe Major.

One year, I invited my wife's parents to be our special guests. At the start of the ceremony, from my eagle's nest commentary position on the Half Moon Battery, I announced: "The Pipes and Drums will march across the drawbridge playing . . ." and as I did so, I saw my father-in-law slip from the back of the VIP enclosure and set off down Castlehill. At the junction of Bank Street and George IV Bridge, he turned left and disappeared into the all-enveloping embrace of Deacon Brodie's Tavern.

Well, I thought, pipes and drums are not for everyone and, after all, my father-in-law, Charles Rhodes, was Yorkshire born and bred. However, with faultless timing, ten minutes before the end, I saw him scuttling back to resume his seat. Later, in the Mess, over a dram, I asked him, "Well, Charles, what did you think of it – did it stir your soul and rouse your spirits?"

He looked at me and smiled: "You know, don't you?"

"Yes," I replied, "and I am never going to let you forget it."

Bagpipe music is as natural to me as is breathing. Perhaps Scots are born with the sound of the bagpipes in their blood. I can't remember ever being far from their magical melancholy. From my earliest years in Edinburgh, we always seemed to be surrounded by pipers; at weddings, sports days, school prize-giving, commemorative events, visits to Auld Reekie by members of the Royal Family, and visits to our school by seriously ermine-robed, sombre City dignitaries.

I attended the Royal High School of Edinburgh and was a member of our Army Combined Cadet Force. We had our own pipe band and I remember once marching proudly behind the band from our school building on the side of Calton Hill, down Regent Road to Holyrood, where we had an open day for parents. My mum and dad were there. They were Scottish Country Dancers and I was soon captivated by that music as well; which is, I suppose, how I came to know Pipe Major Sandy Forbes.

In my mother's later years, she stayed near us at Caladh Sona, a residential home in Melness, across the Kyle from where we live in the township of Tongue. Sandy is a skilled musician and regularly entertained the residents, playing piano, piano accordion and, of course, the pipes. Sandy recognised my mother's love of music and always played her favourite tunes, including the Scottish Country Dance melodies that she loved so much. Sandy brought a lot of joy into her life and when he asked me if I could arrange a day's trout fishing for himself and one of his friends, I was happy to do so.

It was a wonderful outing but when Sandy and his friend tried to pay me for acting as their gillie, I refused even to consider it. But as much as I insisted that it wasn't necessary, so they insisted that it was. In desperation, I struggled to find a solution. It came to me in an inspirational flash. "Sandy," I said, "why don't you just write me a pipe tune instead?" In due course, the tune arrived, a rousing jig which Sandy called "The Bruce", and it is included in his latest book, *The Ben Loyal Collection, Ceòl Beag and Ceòl Mor – Tunes for the Highland Bagpipe*.

Sandy learned to play the pipes as a boy and he served during the war with Royal Armoured Corps. He became a piper in the Seaforth Highlanders and studied under the legendary Pipe Major Willie Ross at the Army School of Piping in Edinburgh Castle. The School was founded in 1910 on the initiative of the Piobaireachd Society. At the age of nineteen, Sandy had the distinction of being the youngest holder of the Pipe Major's Certificate in the British Army. Sandy is a well-known figure in the piping world, at home and abroad, and he has spent a lifetime playing, teaching and judging.

It was through Sandy that I met one of his friends, also a famous figure on the Scottish piping scene, Pipe Major Andrew Venters. Andrew lives at Culloden near Inverness and he is a bright-eyed, sprightly man with an enormous sense of fun and a ready smile. He was born in Edinburgh in 1935, and started his piping career with the Boys Brigade and playing with the Thurso Pipe Band in Caithness in 1948 during a summer camp at Castletown.

Andrew joined the Queen's Own Cameron Highlanders in 1953 with the sole aim of becoming a piper. He told me, "I had played for the Pipe Major and thought that I hadn't done too badly, but I didn't hear any more. Until one day, as we were training on the barrack square, the Pipe Major saw me. "What are you doing there?" he asked. I tried to explain but he said, "Right, you, come wi me, now!" Andrew served in Austria, Germany and Korea before being demobbed from the army in 1956.

Andrew rejoined the army in 1960 and graduated from the Army School of Piping's Pipe Majors course in 1963. After the Cameron and the Seaforth Highlanders were amalgamated, in 1969 Andrew became the regimental Pipe Major. He served and played with the band in Singapore, Borneo and Germany, and toured with them throughout much of Europe and the USA. After leaving the army in 1982, he became the piping instructor to the schools on the Black Isles. He recruited and trained the Black Isles Schools Pipe Band, famous throughout Scotland for its high standard of piping and drumming, and for its immaculate turnout and drill.

Andrew became Pipe Major to the Queen's Own Regimental Association Pipe Band in 1984 and still holds that position in 2011. Like Sandy Forbes, Andrew has also built up a reputation as a composer whose melodies have instant appeal. I was privileged to hear Andrew and five of his companions playing at the Queen's Own Highlanders Pipe and Drums annual dinner in Inverness on St Andrews Night 2010. The programme promised, after dinner, a "Selection of pipe tunes from Pipe Major Andy Venters and others," and it was one of the most memorable and amazing performances of pipe music that I have heard.

The following morning I travelled west, to the Summer Isles and Achiltibuie, to meet one of the world's most renowned and respected pipers, Major Bruce Hitchings, MBE, BEM. Bruce lives with his wife, Alison, and their two boys, Seamus and Finlay, in an isolated house by the sea in Coigach, the "fifth part" part of Ross-shire. Their home is backed by the vast bulk of Ben More Coigach (743m) and looks westwards over the broken waters of the Minch to Skye and the Outer Hebrides. It seemed to me to be an entirely appropriate setting for someone who plays our music with such extraordinary skill and dramatic passion.

Bruce was born in Huntersville on the North Island of New Zealand. His grandfather, a Gunn from Dunnet in Caithness, emigrated to New Zealand during the later years of the nineteenth century, taking with him one of his most prized possessions, a fine set of 1886 MacDougall bagpipes. Bruce revered his grandfather's pipes. He told me, "When I was a boy, I knew that I would be a piper. That is all that I ever really wanted to be." By the age of nine, he was playing with the local band, and by fifteen, with the prestigious City of Wellington Pipe Band.

When the band went to the UK to play in the World Championships in 1975, Bruce went with them, and also on their subsequent tours around the UK and Canada. But when the band returned to New Zealand, Bruce stayed on in Edinburgh to follow the competition circuit and finally, in 1977, to be offered a place in the Black Watch Territorial Army Pipe band. A year later, he enlisted in the Queen's Own Highlanders and in 1979, he won the Silver Medal at the Argyllshire Gathering.

His career in the army encompassed twenty-two years, during which time he served in Northern Ireland and Hong Kong, but in 1980, he was offered a place on the Pipe Major's course at Edinburgh Castle and, by 1986, Bruce was Pipe Major of the Queen's Own Highlanders. As Warrant Officer Class 1, Bruce was the senior pipe major in the British Army and he ended his military career in Edinburgh Castle as the Chief Instructor at the Army School of Piping.

We sat round the kitchen table for lunch, Scotch broth and freshly baked bread served by Bruce's wife Alison. From somewhere around the house, I heard the sound of a chanter. "The boys?" I asked. Alison smiled. "Yes," she replied, "I think that you will understand that they didn't really have any other option. And they love it." Alison herself plays the bagpipes and was Pipe Major of the Ullapool Pipe Band. As a girl, she studied with Andrew Venters at Dingwall High School and has many happy memories of her playing days.

After lunch, Bruce took me to his workshop, where he developed his revolutionary "Balance Tone" drone reeds, now used in bagpipes around the world. The reeds are easily set up, "strike in" every time, take a minimum amount of air, are rock steady and have a telescopic adjustment to alter their pitch. You can find out more about these remarkable reeds by logging on to Bruce's website at: www.highlandreeds.com, where you will also find everything you ever need to know about Highland bagpipes and everything associated with playing them.

Finally, as the sun was setting over the Summer Isles, Bruce showed me the miraculous MacDougall pipes, the ones that his grandfather had taken to New Zealand with him and that had so inspired a young boy that he had devoted the rest of his life to making music with them. I thanked Bruce and Alison for their courtesy and as I got into my car to drive home, I heard again, in the background, above the sound of the wind on the moor, the lyrical cry of a chanter.

9.
Seal Island

On a wild night in December 1938, the last inhabitants of Eilean nan Ron boarded a small boat and set off into the gathering storm. Their destination was Skerray Harbour, one mile distant across the broken seas that constantly torment the north coast of Scotland. Shattered waves drenched them with ice-cold spray as the boat pitched and tossed on the angry waters. The homes that they had left behind them quickly merged into the all-enveloping wall of darkness. Ahead, on the mainland, lights from cottages around Skerray flickered and beckoned. But that night, on the island that they had called home, the lights went out forever.

Eilean nan Ron, more commonly known today as Island Roan, lies in the parish of Tongue in North Sutherland, east of the entrance to the shallow waters and golden sands of the Kyle of Tongue. The Gaelic meaning of the name is "The Island of Seals", because Island Roan is a favoured breeding ground for these mystical creatures. The island is one and a half kilometres long by up to a kilometre wide and it covers an area of 700 acres. The highest point on the island is seventy-five metres above sea level and to the north west, separated by a narrow channel, lies a satellite isle, little Eilean Iosal. The only safe place to land on Island Roan is at Port na h-Uaille, where there is a landing stage from which steps have been cut into the cliff face leading up to the village.

In the early years of the nineteenth century, during the harsh times of the Sutherland Clearances, families trekked north from the fertile straths in which they had lived to the exposed coastal lands overlooking the North Sea. After the Strathnaver evictions in 1819, many of the destitute settled at Skerray, "between the rocks and the sea", and in 1820, four families crossed over to Island Roan to start a new life there. Eventually, the community expanded to more than seventy people and they lived and sustained themselves by fishing and farming, raising sheep and cattle and whatever crops they could grow – oats, hay, potatoes, turnips – on the small, cultivable area of land around which they built their homes.

But by the 1930s, it had become clear that the few people remaining on the island could no longer sustain themselves. The impact of two world wars and the departure of families to the mainland and overseas to Australia, Canada and America, overshadowed the lives of those who remained. This movement of young people away from their homes was mirrored throughout the Highlands of Scotland, when many once-inhabited islands suffered the same fate as Island Roan; also, stocks of fish in the seas around the island, upon which those who lived there relied for food and a source of income, had been badly damaged by the influx of large, modern vessels over-exploiting this finite resource. The lack of able-bodied men to carry out the essential everyday tasks required to exist in such a remote environment meant that, ultimately, evacuation was inevitable.

On a warm morning in October 2009, I set out from Skerray Harbour in search of memories of the people who had lived and loved and thrived on Island Roan and, as the boat headed across the crests of gently rolling waves, sunlight sparkled the sea silver. Graceful gannets, white stars against a blue sky, wheeled and dived for fish. Black shags and busy guillemots bobbed on the surface and as we approached the island, the ruins of the deserted houses were starkly etched above a foreground of ragged, scarred cliffs. I used to work as the archivist for the Skerray Historical Association and was familiar with the history of Island Roan and fascinated by its story. As I looked at the houses, I thought that I caught the scent of peat smoke drifting to greet us.

The people of the island were renowned for the gracious and friendly welcome they always afforded visitors, and this is well documented in a Visitors Book that records these events. The book was maintained from 1883 until 1999 and was gifted to the islanders by Lady Millicent, the Duchess of Sutherland, whose family owned the island then and still do so to this day. The book names the more than 2,500 people who came to Island Roan during these years, to meet friends and relatives or simply to enjoy the peace and serenity that imbued the island. In July 1884, Charles Cooper, from Edinburgh, left this message: "Where's health and happiness? / In places alone? / Or in the humble cottage / On this bare Island Roan."

After 1938, when the island was evacuated, the Visitors Book records the many, many, times that former inhabitants came back to their island: "Donald Mackay of Island Roan" and "Donald P Mackay, Late of Island Roan" in 1961. "George Mackay, Late of Island Roan" in 1962 and in 1963, Helen C Mackay wrote, "Last visit to the island." In July 1968, the Shanks family from near Glasgow left this message: "Island of cliffs, of seagulls and sheep / Happy the day we spent on your braes / Haven of peace where empty crofts keep / Sweet memory of the folk of the old days – Thanks for a golden day. An island whose spell has captured us."

Perhaps, however, the most poignant entry is an account of the "Island Roan Re-Union of Survivors" held at Coldbackie, between Skerray and Tongue, on 15 December 1973. "Tonight we drank a toast to Island Roan and to all its people, wherever they may be." The last entry in the Visitors Book, on 28 September 1999, was written by Williamina Mackay Megally from Canberra, Australia: "A wonderful experience to see the island where I was born – leaving for Australia in 1928."

When I was with the Skerray Historical Association, I was entranced by a series of wonderful black and white photographs of the island. What puzzled me was when they had been taken and by whom, although I suspected that they were for a feature article in a magazine or newspaper. I found the answer in the Visitors Book in an entry dated 12 June 1937: "Ian M Templeton, Scottish Daily Express, Edinburgh Office." I had brought copies of these photographs, the objective being to identify and photograph the houses and places in which these pictures had been taken.

I found the school house, where the last two pupils had been taught by their elder sister, and as I stood where the blackboard had been, I thought of the classroom in the early years of the twentieth century, when eighteen children crowded into the small space, attentive to the careful direction of their teacher. Happily, an account of these days has been written by one of the islanders, the late John George Mackay, who published a booklet in 1962 describing his experiences growing up on the island. It is a marvellous story and in his preface to the work, John George explained:

> My reason for putting in book form the story of Eilean-nan-Ron is to help to preserve the memory of this once prosperous and happy little island.
>
> I was born on the island and spent my childhood and adolescent years there, and now, with old age creeping over me, and having to spend most of my days alone, I often think of those happy times on the island.
>
> Now that the island is desolate and its surviving natives getting fewer and fewer, I feared that soon there would be no one left to recall the old days. The thought grieved me. Why, I said to myself, why allow the memory of my island to die? But then, how was it going to be kept alive? There was no one left capable of writing a history of its habitation.
>
> I knew full well, with my limited education, that I could not do this either. Nevertheless, I decided to try, and I thought, however simply written the book might be, it might serve as a dedication to the memory of the industrious and God-fearing people who spent their lives on the island.

John George Mackay's book admirably achieves the aims that he set himself and it is a delightful account of the life and times of Island Roan. Although the book is out of print at present, you can find the text at: http://www.scottishweb.net/articles/40/1/The-Story-Of-Island-Roan/Page1.html with a forward written by John George's grandson, Stewart Mackay.

I explored the remains of the nine houses, built so laboriously by the islanders, and then walked over the land that they had cultivated to find the huge cave on the north side where the fish they caught were hung up to cure naturally in the salt spray. As I sat on the cliffs above the cave, lulled by the sound of endless waves breaking on the rocky shore, I was overwhelmed by a feeling of profound content. I walked on to the narrow gap separating Island Roan from Eilean Iosal and to the bay at Ann Innis, spiked with sentinel rock stacks springing from the sea like the fingers of an outstretched hand. On the highest point of the island, we were rewarded with a God-like vista of mainland mountains Ben Loyal, Ben Hee, Ben Hope, Arkle, Foinaven and Cranstackie, coloured blue and silver and grey in white shafts of sunlight.

Later, back at the harbour, we threw out anchors and we sat in the stern of the boat with cups of coffee, enjoying the cry of seabirds and the haunting call of curlew. From time to time, a seal's bewhiskered head would surface and survey us with sad-eyed caution. It was hard to leave but the wind was rising. Reluctantly, we recovered the anchors, cleared them of silky purple and brown seaweed and stowed them safely. The noise of the engine reverberated round the high cliffs as we pulled away from the island and headed back towards Skerray Harbour. I watched the old houses fade into the distance and tasted salt spray on my lips; I said a silent prayer for the souls of those who had lived on Island Roan.

Further information: Any visitor to Island Roan is entirely dependent upon the weather. The best time to plan a visit is during the month of June, July and August. But even then, do not be surprised should adverse weather conditions make the journey impossible.

Landing on the island can be awkward, as is ascending the steps up from the harbour up to the cliff top. The steps have not been maintained and should be approached with caution. All of this requires a reasonable degree of fitness and, if in doubt, you should confine your visit to a sail around the island.

Either way, your visit will be eminently memorable. For information about arranging a visit to Island Roan, telephone Jimson's Shop in Skerray, tel: 01641 521445.

10.

Gairloch

September is a good-to-be-alive month in the far north of Scotland. Mountains and moorland resound to the roar of rutting stags, hills are purple-clad with heather, whilst majestic salmon, fish that have survived in Scottish waters since the end of the last Ice Age, surge upstream to their ancestral spawning grounds. Ann and I invariably spend a week away at this time of year, exploring the land we love, and this autumn we decided to revisit Wester Ross, one of the most dramatic and welcoming places in all of Scotland.

One of our objectives was to find Ross-shire's oldest Scots Pine (*Pinus sylvestris*), a tree that was young in the days before the Union of Parliaments in 1707, when Scotland lost its separate identity and joined "the auld enemy", England, to give birth to the United Kingdom. It seemed to be an appropriate thing to do, given that Scotland now has a new government led, for the first time ever, by the Scottish National Party.

We also wanted to explore Loch Maree and historic, tree-clad Isle Maree, one of the many islands that grace this lovely, nineteen-kilometre-long loch; named after St Maelrubha (The Red Priest), the Irish saint who introduced Christianity to the area in 671–673AD. We intended to spend time at Osgood Mackenzie's famous gardens at Inverewe, which contain more than 2,500 species of plants gathered from around the world, and to explore the wild peninsula that lies between Loch Ewe and Loch Gairloch.

Trees have always played an important part in the culture and heritage of Scotland. For instance, a Gaelic verse hails the humble hazelnut as being the source of all knowledge: "Thou nut of my heart / Thou face of my sun / Thou harp of my music / Thou crown of my sense." The same tradition suggested that knowledge could be acquired by eating a salmon caught in a pool surrounded by nine hazel trees.

Our Celtic ancestors revered their natural habitat and, in particular, the oak woods where they worshipped their gods and burned oak in sacred fires. Oak wood was also used to build the boats from which they fished for salmon. Salmon were considered to be a sign of wisdom and were often portrayed on intricately-carved symbol stones.

Remnants of these ancient forests, the Great Wood of Caledon, which covered 90% of Scotland, still survive today but less than 1% remains; by Loch Rannoch in Perthshire, Loch Affric in Inverness-shire, Strathspey, Mar Lodge on Royal Deeside, and around the shores and islands of Loch Maree.

The forests were destroyed to make a way through the woods secure from wolves and robbers, for building dwellings and, significantly, to build warships during the Napoleonic Wars. From 1610 onwards, the trees were burned in the process of producing iron and this is remembered in the names of locations where iron smelting flourished – Bonawe on Loch Etive and at Furnace on the shores of Loch Maree.

Ann and I found our Scots Pine when we followed the Beinn Eighe Mountain Nature Trail up to the skirts of Meall a'Ghiubhais (878m), one of the outriders of the mighty Beinn Eighe range that embraces six Munros – Scottish mountains over 914.4 metres in height – including Sail Mhor (981m) and, the highest point, Ruadh-stac Mor (1010m).

Beinn Eighe is Britain's oldest National Nature Reserve, established in 1951 to protect and preserve the ancient pinewoods near Kinlochewe. The reserve extends to some forty-eight square kilometres and is now owned and managed by Scottish Natural Heritage, the government agency charged with caring for Scotland's precious inheritance of wildlife habitats and landscapes. The aim of the organisation is to help people to enjoy Scotland's natural heritage responsibly, understand it more fully and to use it wisely so that it can be sustained for future generations.

The Beinn Eighe Mountain Nature Trail is not a walk for the faint-hearted and should not be undertaken lightly. You must be properly prepared and dressed for whatever the weather decides to throw at you, and although the trail is less than five kilometres in length, it climbs steeply in places to almost 550 metres. Allow three to four hours for the round trip.

As we descended from the high point of the trail, past Lunar Loch – so named to commemorate man's first landing on the moon on 21 July 1969 and strangely similar to a lunar landscape – we followed the crystal waters of the An t-Allt burn down into the dramatic gorge where the Lone Pine holds court. It is an awesome tree, gnarled and majestic. We sat for a while beneath its branches and told it about the advent of the new parliament, headed at last by those who value Scotland's independence. As we left, I swear that I heard the tree mutter, "And about time, too!"

The main population centre here is the village of Gairloch (the Short Loch) extending to include the neighbouring community of Charlestown. It is a bustling holiday centre where children play on golden sands or splash in clear waters warmed by the Gulf Stream. There are excellent hotels, restaurants, craft centres, an outstanding heritage museum, golf course, pony trekking, hill walking and climbing, sail boarding, organised wildlife safaris, game fishing for salmon, trout and sea-trout, sea fishing and whale-watching trips, stalking and shooting – indeed, something to keep every member of your party well-exercised, amused and happy.

But the shores of the Short Loch were not always so peaceful. Famine and evictions during the nineteenth century brought ruin to the north. When Lowland granaries were full, Highlanders starved. People went barefoot, clothed in discarded meal bags, whilst Free Church ministers appealed to Edinburgh and London in vain for help. Lord Napier, leading a Royal Commission into the unrest in the Highlands in 1882, reported: "A state of misery, of wrong-doing, and patient long suffering, without parallel in the history of our country."

The open-air pulpit of the Free Presbyterian church at Gairloch is a reminder of these sad times, when sheep were preferred to people and old and young alike laboured building roads for Destitution Boards, or accepted the blandishments of Emigration Societies and took ship for the Colonies.

Much of the history of these events can be found in the Gairloch Museum and will give you an overview of how the community coped with these depredations and yet survived to fight another day.

For our visit, we found a comfortable self-catering cottage in the straggling crofting township of Melvaig – about seven miles to the north of Gairloch along the narrow, tortuous road that leads out to Rua Reidh Lighthouse. Our cottage overlooked the sea and was within a couple of hundred yards of the nearest beach. The views were magnificent and sunsets an unforgettable joy – westwards, beyond the Shiant Isles, to the long islands of Lewis, Harris, North Uist, Benbecula and South Uist in the Outer Hebridies; south west to the Island of Skye, dominated by the stark outline of the Trotternish Ridge – an enduring fusion of light and time and space.

We drove out to the white tower of Rua Reidh Lighthouse, perched precariously above the broken waters of the Minch, guarded by myriads of endlessly wheeling gulls. Rua Reidh offers simple, inexpensive accommodation and when we arrived, a young couple were waiting to book in. They were from Spain, engaged to be married and as much in love with the Scottish landscape as they were clearly in love with each other.

The following morning, Ann and I set sail for Isle Maree. Our guide was Nick Thompson and we met Nick at the Loch Maree Hotel. The hotel used to be one of the most famous fishing hotels in Europe because of the quality of the sea-trout fishing on the loch. Each season, from March to September, anglers could catch upwards of 1,500 sea-trout in Loch Maree, as well as good numbers of salmon. Tragically, because of disease and pollution from fish farms, sea-trout and salmon numbers have collapsed in recent years and the hotel has closed its doors to anglers.

However, because of the scenic beauty of the loch and the historical importance of Isle Maree, Nick spends much of his time during the year taking parties out to the island. The story of the island is as much myth as it is factual but it is probable that in Celtic times Isle Maree was revered as being a sacred isle, dedicated to Rhiannon, the Celtic goddess of the moon. It was definitely the site of pagan rituals, as there are records of bulls being sacrificed there well into the seventeenth century.

What is beyond dispute, however, is the date of the "druid circle", which is one of the most remarkable features of the island. According to archaeological research, it has been dated at around 100 BC. The Vikings also knew the island: two graves, reputedly of a prince and princess thwarted in love, lie within the stone circle and show an inscription that may depict a Viking axe. Oak trees abound on Isle Maree, as well as holly, birch and beech, but, strangely, few birds sing. Tradition also notes that anybody who removes anything from the island will meet with a serious, if not fatal, accident.

There is also the "money tree", close to the ruins of Saint Maelrubha's cell and the site of the long-since-vanished "sacred well". Exactly when visitors to the island began the practice of hammering coins into the trunk of the tree is not clear but the oldest coin has been dated at 1828. The wish made whilst fixing the stone would be granted, provided that the coin remained in place and did not fall out. When Queen Victoria visited Isle Maree in 1877, she also left behind a coin in the tree.

We left Isle Maree and on our way back to the mooring bay, we passed amongst the other islands on the loch, Eilean Subhainn, Eilean Ruairidh Mor, Garbh Eilean and Eilean Dubh na Sroine. They were very lovely, also tree-clad and some with amazing, white sand beaches, but none had that special feeling which I had experienced on Isle Maree. It was not a feeling that evoked fear or anguish; the reverse was the case, it was a feeling of happiness. Later, as we talked about our day, Ann said that she also experienced a sense of calmness as she walked amongst the ancient stones on this enchanted isle.

Inverewe Gardens are much more organised than Isle Maree but none-the-less engaging and special for being so. We spent our last afternoon exploring the 100-acre gardens, adjudged by many to be one of the finest gardens in the world. As evening slowly silvered the sky, we watched the changing light play on the black Boor Rocks in Loch Ewe, whilst, in the distance, the gathering darkness shrouded the mighty Beinn Eighe peaks in mystery and settled them to rest.

For Melvaig self-catering properties see: http://www.cottageshighlands.com; for other accommodation see: http://www.celticfringe.org.uk/gairloch-breakfast.htm; to arrange boat trips to Isle Maree, call Nick Thompson at the Loch Maree Hotel on tel: 01445 760288; for further information about the Beinn Eighe National Nature Reserve, see: http://www.snh.org.uk or contact the Reserve Visitor Centre on tel: 01445 760254 during working hours.

11.
Scottish Regiments

Clan Mackay and Clan Sutherland fought their last battle in 1431 at Druim na Coup on the northern slopes of Ben Loyal. I see the site from my window as I write and, sometimes, when I walk that way, I think I hear the cry of angry voices. But it is the rush of the wind across the moor echoing amidst the corners and corries of the mountain.

We Scots are a warlike race. From the Borders to the Shetland Isles, hardly a square inch of my native soil is free from association with some deadly struggle. But the carnage of Culloden on 14 April 1746 destroyed the warrior clans. Their land was stolen and they became the tenants and slaves of their English-educated lairds. To enhance their own dignity and impress London society, the lairds raised companies of soldiers – led, of course, by the lairds themselves.

Out of these beginnings, many Scottish regiments were born. It is not unreasonable to suggest that without the fighting quality of the Scottish soldier, Britain could never have sustained its far-flung Empire. They played a major role in protecting the commercial interests of the nation, often at terrible cost to themselves. The story of their battles, triumphs and disasters is one of astonishing courage, vividly told in regimental museums throughout the land.

Edinburgh is a good starting point for a journey of military discovery. I was born and brought up in Auld Reekie and by the time I was ten years old, I was convinced that it was my solemn duty to die, not in bed, but on the battlefield. My maternal grandfather was a Drum Major in the Royal Scots and he survived the carnage of Flanders Fields during the First World War. Joining the school Army Cadet Force was the natural thing to do. I was proud to be associated with our parent regiment, the Royal Scots, whose badge we wore.

The regimental museum is in Edinburgh Castle, where, above the entrance, after crossing the drawbridge, are written the words, "Nemo me impune lacessit" – nobody harasses me with impunity or, to put it in broad Scots, wha dar meddle wi me. The Regimental cap badge, one of which I still have and treasure, has the figure of St Andrew, worn with a red felt backing.

The Royal Scots Museum in the Castle was opened in June 1991 by the Colonel in Chief of the Regiment, HRH The Princess Royal. As a youth, I used to haunt Edinburgh Castle and there is no more appropriate place to read the history of the city's famous regiment. This proud regiment is the oldest in the British Army and takes precedence by being on the right of the line on parade.

There has always been rivalry between Scotland's two major cities, Edinburgh and Glasgow, but there is no dispute about the courage of the Glasgow Regiment, the Royal Highland Fusiliers, Princess Margaret's Own Glasgow and Ayrshire Regiment; a core of which was originally employed in 1678 to keep "Watch on the Braes" to suppress Highland lawlessness.

One of the best known soldiers of the Royal Scots Fusiliers was Lt Col Winston Churchill. In 1915, the future Second World War leader commanded the 6th Battalion of the Regiment at Ploegsteert, called "Plug Street" by the soldiers, in the hellhole that was the Ypres Salient. Churchill earned respect by leading his men into battle and survived thirty-six forays across no man's land. He is reputed to have said later: "Although an Englishman, it was in Scotland that I found the best things in my life – my wife, my constituency and my Regiment."

Stirling Castle is one of Scotland's most dramatic fortifications, dominating the flat lands that enfold the River Forth and Flanders Moss. It has played a central role in Scotland's story and is the home of the Argyll and Sutherland Highlanders Regimental Museum. The regiment was formed in 1881 when the 91st Argyllshire Highlanders and the 93rd Sutherland

Highlanders were amalgamated as Princess Louise's Argyllshire and Sutherland Highlanders.

The 93rd were raised in Strathnaver in Sutherland by Elizabeth, Countess of Sutherland, in 1799, primarily by coercion; families unwilling to give up their men faced almost certain eviction from the land they rented from the Countess. In the event, it didn't really matter, because a few years later the Countess, who had promised the soldiers' families her protection "for all time coming" evicted them anyway to make way for sheep farming.

The history of both regiments is displayed in Stirling Castle's museum. The 91st first saw action at Cape of Good Hope and later played a major part in the Peninsular Wars when it protected Sir John Moore's retreat to Corunna. The regiment was demoralized, however, when, in 1809, it lost the right to wear the kilt, adjudged at the time to be "objectionable to the natives of South Britain".

The members of the 93rd were revered for their self-discipline and firmly held religious beliefs. They gained great honour during the Battle of New Orleans when, under appalling leadership, they stood firm amidst fire from General Andrew Jackson's defending force, suffering 557 casualties in the process out of a total for the defeated army of 2,000. The Americans had six men killed and seven wounded.

Perhaps the most famous moment for the 93rd came when they formed the "Thin Red Line" at the Battle of Balaclava in 1854 during the Crimean War. Standing in line, two deep, they faced a furious charge by Russian cavalry. Sir John Campbell, their commander, called: "There is no retreat from here, men, you must die where you stand."

"Aye, Sir John. And needs be we'll do that."

The line held, and their courage and fortitude broke the charge and saved the day.

Am Freiceadan Dubh, the Black Watch, have their regimental base in the fair city of Perth by the swiftly-flowing River Tay. Balhousie Castle, built in 1860 and incorporating an earlier, sixteenth-century L-plan tower house, was acquired by the Army after the Second World War and in 1962, the castle became the Black Watch regimental headquarters and museum.

The force was raised in 1729 in an attempt to subdue discontent amongst the mainly Catholic Highland clans, caused when a Protestant, William of Orange, usurped the Catholic King James in 1688. The young men who flocked to join the new independent units were called the "Black Watch" to distinguish them from regular troops, the Saighdearan Dearg, or "Red Soldiers", because of their red uniforms.

These independent companies soon proved their worth and were amalgamated into a single regiment on the outbreak of war with Spain in 1730. This coming-together was carried out on the Birks of Aberfeldy between Tay Bridge and Aberfeldy in Perthshire. The new force was designated as the 43rd (Highland) Regiment but they are still known to this day as the Black Watch.

The regiment fought bravely in 1815, facing and defeating the full might of Marshal Ney's 2nd French Army cavalry charges. They distinguished themselves at the Battle of Alma in 1854 in the Crimean War, and fought with honour and courage in the wars and skirmishes leading up to the Boer Wars and the Great World Wars of the twentieth century. Memorials of these times – medals, uniforms, equipment and mementoes – adorn the museum.

The last part of our military journey takes us north east from Perth to the Granite City of Aberdeen on the cold shores of the North Sea – the home of the museum of the Gordon Highlanders, raised in 1794 by the 4th Duke of Gordon. The regiment draws its strength from Aberdeenshire, Kincardine and Morayshire and to encourage men to join the regiment, it is said that each recruit was kissed by the Duchess of Gordon herself.

The regiment fought alongside the Black Watch at the Battle of Les Quatre Bras in 1815 and they were so eager to engage with the enemy at Waterloo that many soldiers clung to horse-riders' stirrups to speed their progress into battle. As Britain's Empire flourished during the nineteenth century, the Gordons saw action in India, Egypt and the Sudan, and in South

Africa during the Boer Wars. During the nightmare of the First World War, the Gordons, out of a total complement of 50,000 men, lost 27,000 killed or wounded in the conflict.

Their regimental museum in Aberdeen displays a unique collection of artifacts, including twelve Victoria Crosses won by members of the regiment. The museum also has an audio-visual theater showing an absorbing film of the history and activities of the regiment. And, for children, a "handling area" where boys and girls can dress in Gordon Highland uniforms and wear the equipment that soldiers had to carry.

There are other, equally famous Scottish regiments, each with their rightful place in Scotland's military history and each celebrated and remembered in individual regimental museums: the Scots Guards (Birdcage Walk, London), the King's Own Scottish Borders (Berwick upon Tweed), the Cameronians (Hamilton), the Queen's Own Highlanders (Fort George, near Inverness).

And there are more personal, poignant reminders of Scotland's soldiers in every Scottish community: the poppy-bedecked, inscribed memorials that commemorate the ultimate sacrifice tens of thousands of my fellow Scots made during two World Wars. Across the Kyle of Tongue from my home is a tiny graveyard with one such memorial. It stands on a green hill by the shore. Gulls cry and curlew call over the sleeping bodies gathered there, home at last.

The museums noted above can all be visited during the course of a single week. Edinburgh is an excellent centre from which to do so, by train or bus. Auld Reekie also offers a full range of other activities to keep every member of your party amused whilst you journey through Scottish military history.

Further details and opening times from:

The Royal Scots Regimental Museum, The Castle, Edinburgh EH1 2YT. Tel: 0131 310 5016; Fax: 0131 310 5019; email: rhqrs@btconnect.com

The Royal Highland Fusiliers, 518 Sauchiehall Street, Glasgow G2 3LW. Tel: 0141 332 5639; email: reg.sec@rhf.org.uk

Argyll and Sutherland Highlanders Regimental Museum, The Castle, Stirling FK8 1EH. Tel: 01786 475165; Fax: 01786 446038; email: museum@argylls. co.uk

The Black Watch Regimental Museum, Balhousie Castle, Hay Street, Perth PH1 5HS. Tel: 0131 310 8530; Fax: 0131 310 8525; email: rhq@theblackwatch. co.uk

The Gordon Highlanders Regimental Museum, St Luke's, Viewfield Road, Aberdeen AB15 7XH. Tel: 01224 311200; email: museum@gordonhighlanders. com

12.
An Island For All Seasons

Islay — pronounced "I-la" — is a speck on God's great map. People from this tiny island, a two-hour sail from the jagged west coast of Argyllshire, have flourished in the four quarters of His planet but they never lose their love for "The Queen of the Hebrides", the fertile island that they call home.

I thought of these truths as I waited with Ann at Kennacraig on the Mull of Kintyre for the arrival of the Caledonian MacBrayne ferry to Islay. Flying is not for me. The best way to arrive on a Scottish island is by sea, as our ancestors did. Caledonian MacBrayne's fleet of ships is the heartbeat of the Hebrides, as a well-known West Coast rhyme reminds us,

> The Earth belongs unto the Lord
> And all that it contains,
> Except the Clyde and Western Isles,
> They're Caledonian MacBrayne's.

It had taken us seven hours to drive from North Sutherland to the ferry, built on Eilean Ceann na Creige, an islet connected to the mainland by a causeway. I walked to the pier-head to stretch my legs. It was a grey afternoon with a grey mist on the sea's face and a grey evening breaking. A flight of geese arrowed by in perfect formation. An ink-black cormorant dived for supper in the waters of West Loch Tarbert.

As I watched, a brown-bewhiskered head appeared above the waves. Dark, shining eyes gazed up at me. It was a dog otter, going about its lawful business, curious and unafraid. He swam towards me until only a few yards away. Did he smile and bid me welcome? I think so and I knew then that we were going to experience all that is finest about Scotland's islands when we crossed the sea to Islay.

The island offers something for every member of your tribe, young and old alike. For Clan Sandison, it is a complete paradise encompassing all that we love: unspoiled, yellow-sand beaches washed by white-topped green waves; golden moors guarded by hen harrier, buzzard and golden eagle; wonderful trout lochs and streams where salmon lie; myriad dragonflies, wild flowers and butterflies, including the rare Marsh Fritillary (*Eurodryas aurinia*); cliff-top walks and kindly hills that beckon.

Islay is also famous for whisky distilleries, all of which welcome visitors. There are seven, giving the chance of sampling a different dram each day of the week. They are: Caol Ila, Bunnahabhain, Bruichladdich, Bowmore, Ardbeg, Lagavulin and Laphroaig. I particularly liked Caol Ila, light-coloured and comforting, which I had never tasted before. The distillery stands in a sheltered cove close to Port Askaig. David Graham of the Ballygrant Inn, over a pint, told me a tale about two regular Caol Ila visitors.

"Duncan MacGregor, whose father was gamekeeper on Dunlossit Estate, was friendly with crew members of the *Loch Ard*, a trading vessel that called at Port Askaig. The captain of the *Loch Ard* was known as 'Polaris' because he always steered a straight course and Duncan used to take Polaris and the ship's engineer, 'Paraffin Dan', to the Caol Ila distillery to stock up with whisky for the crew. [I hesitated to ask how Paraffin Dan came by his name.]

"In those days, distillery workers were given two drams of clear spirit a day. Polaris and Paraffin Dan just joined the end of the queue. When their turn came, the jug containing the whisky was often less than empty because the brewer invariably filled it too full. After the other men had gone back to work, the brewer disposed of the surplus into lemonade bottles brought by Polaris and Paraffin Dan for that purpose – much to their shipmates' delight on a cold night at sea."

The distilleries are as distinctive for their appearance as they are for the wonderful quality of the malt whisky that they produce. It is almost as though, before dawn each morning, a team of cleaners brush and polish the premises from top to bottom. They are pristine, shining white and none more so than Bowmore Distillery by the colourful, boat-bobbing little harbour in the town that gave it its name.

Bowmore is the oldest Islay distillery and it has graced the shores of shallow Loch Indaal since 1779. It is one of the few remaining distilleries in Scotland that still produces its own malt barley, hand-turned on the floor by the Maltman using traditional wooden malt shovels. The whisky is stored in damp vaults below sea level in Spanish and American oak casks that give the whisky its distinctive mellow flavor – maturing it into a dream-like, marvelous, memorable drinking experience.

Bowmore has a magnificent, wide, main street dominated by the Round Church (1769). The oldest houses are between the Harbour Inn and the Pier. They have external stairs to the upper floors. House and shop fronts are painted in various colours, with the dominant colour being white. Another dominant aspect of Main Street is one of Scotland's most inviting bakeries, "The Bakery", where bread and scones and other delights are baked on the premises. The smell alone is reason enough to linger and the bread is to die for.

Islay exudes self-confidence and this is evident from the way in which properties, like the distilleries, are maintained. It seems to be a matter of a community pride, rather than official dictate, that has achieved this standard. This "philosophy" perhaps reaches its highest expression in the Rinns, the most westerly part of Islay. You will find here two of the most attractive villages in all of Scotland, Port Charlotte and Portnahaven, both amazingly lovely and welcoming.

Also amazing is the wind. As we walked the Big Strand Beach one afternoon, along the shore of Laggan Bay south from Bowmore, the wind was so fierce that it lifted the sand and sent it flying like a white wave before us. The sea was in constant turmoil, meeting the sky in a fury of blue and green foam. But by the following morning, the storm had passed and we hurried north to visit the Loch Gruinart Nature Reserve in search of the geese that make Islay as famous as its whisky.

The Royal Society for the Protection of Birds (RSPB) bought the reserve in 1984 and 45% of the world's population of Greenland barnacle geese come to Loch Gruinart during the winter months. There is an excellent Visitor Centre at Aoradh Farm, which the RSPB runs as a model example of environmentally-friendly agriculture. A few hundred yards north, a track leads down to the shore of Loch Gruinart to a splendid bird-watching "hide", accessed by a sunken track so that approaching visitors can't be seen by the birds.

The hide has windows overlooking the fields that border the loch and a more than adequate supply of books to help you identify the different species. When Ann and I arrived, in mid-October, we were confronted by a spectacular display: 20,000 barnacle geese, more than 1,000 white-fronted geese, Canada geese, brent geese, wigeon, teal, mallard, shoveler, pintail, pochard, long-tailed duck, goldeneye, a pair of statuesque herons, and even a brace of brightly-plumed pheasant. It was one of the most unforgettable sights that I have ever seen and the music the birds made was a miraculous symphony of sheer delight.

Another rare Islay bird, the chough, a member of the crow family with a distinctive red beak, proved more difficult to find. Accompanied by an invigorating wind, we walked the RSPB reserve at the Oa on the south-west coast of Islay in search of it and were rewarded by a brief glimpse of a pair cart-wheeling in the storm. However, the dominant feature here is the American Monument, on the edge of the cliffs on the headland at Mull of Oa. It was built by the United States Government to commemorate the 266 Americans who drowned when the *HMS Tuscania* was torpedoed by a German submarine ten miles offshore on 5 February 1918. The bodies of some of those who died lie at rest in a small graveyard close to the ruins of Kilnaughton Chapel to the west of Port Ellen.

Being an angler, I visited Loch Finlaggan near Ballygrant. Only one salmon has ever been caught in Finlaggan and that was taken in 1930 by one of Scotland's best-loved song writers and comedians, Sir Harry Lauder. But the real treasures here are the tiny islands at the north end of Finlaggan,

Eilean na Comhairle (The Council Isle) and Eilean Mor (The Great Isle). From these inconspicuous sites, the Lords of the Isles, Clan MacDonald, ruled a vast, independent kingdom for nearly 400 years.

But evidence from excavations at Finlaggan has shown that people lived there long before the Lordship of the Isles; Eilean Mor is a natural island but Eilean na Comhairle and another island off the east shore are in fact crannogs, man-made islets that could date back to Neolithic times (4000–2000 BC). As we explored the islands, in my imagination I saw these people netting the loch for trout, smelled the smoke from their cooking fires and heard the laughter of their children at play.

In all of my travels round Scotland, I have rarely come across anywhere else that is as visitor-friendly as Islay. The Ileachs make you welcome and try hard to ensure that your stay amongst them is enjoyable and enriching. Our last day found us in the north of Islay, where we discovered a heavenly, deserted beach, Traigh Baile Aonghais. The sea was calm and autumn sunlight warmed our walk. It was hard to leave. Islay is an enduring joy, an island for all seasons.

For further information about Islay, contact the Islay Development Company, Distillery Road, Port Ellen, Islay PA43 7JX; Tel: 01496 300010; Email: info@ islay.org.uk

For ferry information and bookings, contact: Caledonian MacBrayne Limited, Ferry Terminal, Gourock PA19 1QP; Tel: 01475 650100; Email: enquiries@ calmac.co.uk; Website: www.calmac.co.uk

For information about the RSPB Loch Gruinart Reserve, contact RSPB Loch Gruinart Reserve, Bushmills Cottage, Gruinart, Bridgend, Isle of Islay, Argyll PA44 7PR; Tel: 01496 850505; Email: loch.gruinart@rspb.org.uk; Website: www.rspb.org.uk

13.
Lerwick Ablaze

The night sky was starless. A Presbyterian wind buffeted me and it was raining hard. I hunched into my waterproof jacket, captivated by the mounting excitement. Suddenly, a signal rocket was launched, splashing the darkness red as more than 800 torches were lit and held aloft by the members of forty-six squads of local people, nearly 1,000 participants, waiting for the arrival of the Guizer Jarl and his helpers. Viking axes, horned-helmets and studded shields sparkled in the glow. Everyone cheered. It was 7.30pm in Lerwick, Shetland, on Tuesday, 28 January 2003, and the highlight of "Up Helly Aa" had begun: the ceremonial burning of a nine-metre-long Viking Galley.

Earlier, Niall Cruickshank, a storyteller and singer, had explained the importance of Up Helly Aa. "Celebration in the winter time has always been part of Shetland life. The winters are lang and dark. In the past, this was when people repaired their fishing nets and agricultural implements and in the evenings, they gathered together in somebody's house, to tell stories, play music and sing. From Norse times, Christmas was a twenty-four-day celebration because there was precious little else to do. Up Helly Aa has always been associated with fire, and dressing up and disguising yourself and visiting friends."

Up Helly Aa was also important because it chased away Trolls – supernatural, heathen goblins, little people who lived in the hills. On that night of the year, Trolls were free to roam, to steal people's milk and food, and even to kidnap children. A cross made of straw pinned to the front door helped to ward them off. Young men would make and wear a straw skirt, cape and hat to frighten the Trolls. The use of fire and dressing up scared the

Trolls back to their caves and it was out of these beginnings that the present-day festival evolved.

In nineteenth-century Lerwick, it is recalled that, "Sometimes two tubs were fastened to a great raft-like frame knocked together at the Docks, whence combustibles were generally obtained. Two chains were fastened to the bogie supporting the tub or tar barrel . . . eked [joined] to those were strong ropes on which a motley mob, wearing masks for the most part, fastened. A party of about a dozen men stirred up the molten contents to keep them burning." Matters frequently got out of hand and Lerwick jail was often full the morning after. Eventually, it became difficult for the town to enlist sufficient Special Constables to deal with the riots.

The name "Guizer" comes from this tradition of dressing up, of disguising oneself, and it is a great honour to be the Guizer Jarl. Alex Johnson, a chemist, holds the position this year and he posted his personal three-metre-high "Proclamation" at the Market Cross to announce his ascendancy. This is full of personal humour and wit, specifically written to entertain the people of Lerwick. Up Helly Aa is a local tradition, not a spectacle mounted for visitors, although, of course, visitors are well entertained, as I found out over a few drams.

The Guizer Jarl is granted the freedom of the town for Up Helly Aa day and his Raven Banner is flown from the Town Hall. He takes a Viking name for the ceremony; Alex Johnson choosing Olaf Sitricson – Olaf of the Sandals – a tenth-century Viking who commanded a fleet of 600 longships in an effort to expand Norse influence south of Shetland and who eventually died on the island of Iona in 981. A Junior Up Helly Aa festival, with pupils from Anderson High School, is held in tandem with the adult event, when a smaller, six-metre galley is burned two hours before the start of the senior "Burning". This year's Junior Jarl is Shane Jamieson, who took the Viking name of Magnus of Marasetr, a Danish settler who lived on the Island of Whalsay. Before a battle, Magnus, for safety, threw a gold ropework ring amongst his horses. In 1903, a gold ropework ring was found at Marasetr by one of Junior Jarl's ancestors.

The night before, I had visited the Galley Shed where the longship had been built. The final colour of the boat is kept a closely guarded secret until it appears in public. Shields adorn the sides of the boat and round the walls of the Galley Shed are paintings of previous Jarls in scenes from Norse times – longships coming ashore, battles and raids. Bruce Leask, Guizer Jarl in 2002, explained the significance of the shields. "The first shield has a cartoon drawing of the Guizer Jarl, the second shows his seal. Tomorrow is going to be excellent. Regardless of the weather, we always have a great day. The ceremony will never die. Up Helly Aa will never die." I asked Billy Goudie, Guizer Jarl in 2001, if the Up Helly Aa tradition was flourishing: "Younger ones are coming up through the ranks all the time and starting to take over. Lots of people who used to live in Shetland come home for Up Helly Aa."

The following morning, I watched as the galley, named "Aaksytrik" this year and gleaming white, finally arrived at the British Legion Club premises. It looked far too precious for immolation. School children with their teachers began to line the street. The Lerwick Brass Band formed up, ready to begin. Police stopped traffic. The Guizer Jarl and his party emerged from the Legion building and took up position around the galley – sheep-skin cloaked, hugely bearded, brandishing axes, their helmets sparkling in the morning sun. Shops and offices emptied. With three cheers, they were off, striding along Commercial Street towing the galley, the brass band leading. As they passed, members of the squad called for more cheers: "Three cheers for the man on the roof," "Three cheers for the bus station!"

It was a happy day, full of laughter and good humour. The Junior Jarl Squad was royally entertained for lunch by Captain Wheeler of the NorthLink Ferry vessel *MV Hjaltland*, whilst the Guizer Jarl and his squad visited Lerwick schools, the hospital and residential homes. In the afternoon, I enjoyed a concert of music and song, Fiery Sessions, presented by local people at the Garrison Theatre. Now, at 7.30pm precisely, as I watched the signal rocket burst, it was time for the torchlight procession to begin. And it was still raining, if anything even harder. But nothing seemed to dampen the spirits of the torch bearers waiting to accompany the galley to its fate.

They were lined up on either side of the road below the Town Hall, singing in the rain. The Guizer Jarl and his team marched down the ranks through a stream of flame and the whole procession counter-marched, falling in behind them, the Lerwick Brass Band again leading. As the formation moved off, they sang the "The Up Helly Aa Song", learned by every Shetland child at school:

> Grand old Vikings ruled upon the ocean vast,
> Their brave battle-songs still thunder on the blast;
> Their wild war-cry comes a-ringing from the past;
> We answer it "A-oi!"
> Roll their glory down the ages,
> Sons of warriors and sages,
> When the fight for Freedom rages,
> Be bold and strong as they!

The final resting place of the galley was the centre of the King George V Playing Field and the procession followed a circuitous path to reach it. From my vantage point I could see most of the route. The squads filled the street from side to side, sparks flying from their torches, faces aglow with excitement. Fathers hoisted little ones aloft to give them a better view. The ribbon of flame reached the north entrance to the park and filed in to surround the galley. A circle of fire encompassed the vessel. The Guizer Jarl mounted his galley for the last time, axe aloft. Another signal rocket burst overhead and all the Guizers roared out "The Galley Song":

> Floats the raven banner o'er us,
> Round our Dragon Ship we stand,
> Voices joined in gladsome chorus,
> Raised aloft the flaming brand.
> Bonds of Brotherhood inherit,
> O'er strife the curtain draw;

Let our actions breathe the spirit
Of our grand Up-Helly-A'.

A bugle call echoed through the night and the Guizer Jarl rejoined his companions. As the last note sounded, they began to hurl their torches into the galley, spiraling upwards then falling into the doomed vessel in a sheet of startling brightness. One by one, the other squads moved forward to add their torches to the inferno. The sail of the galley was ablaze, the proud figurehead alight. Slowly, the mast tumbled and the Raven Flag was laid low. As the vessel burned, the thousands-strong crowd roared their approval and tension was tangible. The spell was broken as a glorious firework display set the very sky itself afire.

Up Helly Aa celebrations continue well into the next day. Immediately after the Burning, each of the forty-six squads visit eleven private parties in Lerwick community halls to perform a topical sketch, sing a song, dance, drink and celebrate. If visitors wish to join one of these parties, they simply ask the party hostess for permission to do so. Otherwise, they may prefer to enjoy the many lively gatherings in Lerwick hotels and pubs: nobody goes to bed on Up Helly Aa night. But my enduring Up Helly Aa memory is of watching the wonderful torchlight procession and witnessing the proud end of that magnificent, shining white galley – and Up Helly Aa must work, because, you know, I never once saw a single Troll.

14.
Practise Your Swing in Scotland

Like most Scots, I was born with a golf club in my hand. The game is one of Scotland's most popular participant sports. We Jocks have been bashing various designs of golf balls around since the twelfth century. In the time of King James II (1430–1460), the game so captivated the nation that it was banned because it interfered with archery practice and other more urgent military pursuits. The preferred golfing venue in the Middle Ages was Leith Links near Edinburgh, conveniently close to the Scottish Parliament Buildings in the High Street; Scotland's political luminaries, judiciary and the like, could comfortably draft their laws and edicts in the morning and still have plenty of time for a hack round the links before supper.

The world's oldest golf club is the Honourable Company of Edinburgh Golfers. They played their first competition on Leith Links in 1744, one year before Bonnie Prince Charlie arrived in town to temporarily disrupt their swing. Ten years later, twenty-two good-men-and-true in St Andrews formed what has become known as the Royal & Ancient (R&A). They subscribed to the purchase of a silver golf club, to be played for in competition, the winner becoming the club captain for the next year. In recognition of the winner's achievement, a silver ball inscribed with his name was attached to the club. To this day, as a mark of respect, newly elected R&A members at their inaugural dinner are required to kiss the captain's balls.

Two of my most unnerving golfing experiences occurred on two of Scotland's most famous courses. The first was on the Old Course at St Andrews on a cold morning when tee-off time was 9.28am, precisely. I was so over-awed by the occasion that I could barely balance the ball on the tee. The second happened at Old Prestwick, where the first Open Championship was played in 1860. By the time I reached the 9th hole, I had lost nine balls in the unforgiving rough bordering the narrow fairways. As I courageously prepared to address the ball on the 10th tee, my caddie muttered to me: "Och, Sir, this is nae a course for beginners." Still, I did manage a par at the 18th and thus ended the round shaken, with my honour shredded but relatively intact.

This is why I now play most of my golf north of the Great Glen. Golf in the Highlands is much less of a "goldfish bowl" experience than on southern courses such as St Andrews, Carnoustie, Gleneagles, Troon or Turnberry. It is also a lot less expensive, more readily available and, although I admit to being biased, a lot more fun. I have often played round Durness, in North West Sutherland, without meeting another soul. The most taxing hole is a 7 iron shot across the Atlantic. The tee is perched on basalt cliffs above the sea and golfers play over a scallop-shaped inlet, known in these airts as a "geo".

A local man playing this hole recently struck his tee-shot superbly. The ball soared over the geo, bounced on the edge of the green and rolled into the cup. A rare hole-in-one, whereupon he turned to his companion on the tee and announced somberly, "Well, Hamish, you have got this for the half," meaning that his opponent couldn't win, but could even the score if he also managed to get a hole-in-one. The story may be apocryphal, but it encapsulates the way in which the noble game is played in Scotland – with no holds barred; a gentleman's game, yes, but one which gentlemen and ladies play to win.

I should also confess that this delightful little course has another attraction for me apart from the "shot across the Atlantic". The 6th hole borders what is, in my view, one of the finest wild brown trout lochs in Europe. So I sometimes pack a fishing rod in my golf bag and have a few casts along the way.

Another of my favourite courses is at Reiss near Wick in Caithness, a traditional Scottish "links" course sheltered from cold east winds by high sand dunes. Wick Golf Club claims to be the oldest club in the north of Scotland and a new club house, built at a cost of £250,000, was opened in 1994. The 18th tee is one of the most dramatic from which I have ever duffed a drive. It is set high on the sand-dunes bordering the blue and gold sweep of Sinclair Bay and dominated by the tall, gaunt fortress of Ackergill Tower, where Oliver Cromwell's officers were billeted during the religious wars of the seventeenth century, when they brought their Protestant army north to subdue un-Christian-like mirth and jollity.

The newest Highland course, officially opened in April 1998, is at Ullapool in Wester Ross, although there is mention of a golf course at Ullapool as far back as 1903. The present course, designed by Souters of Stirling, took two years to construct and was built by Messrs ATF Urquhart. Ullapool is a busy fishing port and a hub of activity during the summer months. The course lies on a raised beach close to the sea by the banks of the Ullapool River. The surrounding scenery is magnificent with splendid views north west to Isle St Martin and the Summer Isles, and south over Loch Broom to Beinn Ghobhlach (635m) and the hamlet of Altnaharrie, once famous for the food and comfort of its Inn.

Just as famous, although for an entirely different reason, is Fortrose & Rosemarkie Golf Club on the Black Isle to the north of the City of Inverness. The course looks south over the Moray Firth to Fort George – built in the years after the 1745 Rebellion to help "quell" any future Scottish-based insurrection. Before the Second World War, officers stationed at Fort George were given honorary membership of the club. Bandmaster Rickets of Fort George used to play Fortrose & Rosemarkie regularly with his colonel. On one occasion, another player tried to attract the colonel's attention by "whistling" to him. Rickets later used the sounds made in a tune he composed that became internationally renowned as "Colonel Bogey".

North of Inverness, up the busy A9 road, brings you to further golfing delights, not the least of which is Royal Dornoch, where golf was being played as long ago as 1616. This Sutherland links course ranks in the top ten of British courses. Some of the most noted names in golf are associated with Royal Dornoch: Ben Cranshaw, Tom Watson, Greg Norman, Nick Faldo and HRH the Duke of York, who is an honorary member. Another new course is at Skibo Castle, once the home of multi-millionaire Andrew

Carnegie, now a prestigious watering-hole for the world's rich and famous. But I am more concerned here with the less well-known courses and one of the finest in Sutherland is Brora Links.

The Brora golf course, established in 1891, was re-designed in 1923 by James Baird (1870–1950), five-time winner of the Open Championship. Baird won his first title at Muirfield in 1901. He is credited with being involved with the design of more than 180 courses, including the King's Course at Gleneagles and the medal course at Carnoustie. Baird's fee for re-designing the Brora course was £25 and Brora is now the home of "The James Baird Golfing Society", formed in 1997 by Peter Thomson, another five-time winner of the Open Championship. A room at the Royal Marine Hotel in Brora is given over to memorabilia of the great man and the test of Baird's course lies in some wonderful holes: the 13th, "The Snake", with its little burn flowing below the tee; the 15th, "Sahara"; and the spectacular 17th, "Tarbatness", where the lighthouse gives the line to follow.

The beauty of the far north of Scotland, with its grand mountains, heather moorlands, foaming rivers and peat-stained lochs, is extolled throughout the world. Less well known is the fact that it is also a golfer's paradise. Apart from the courses I have mentioned, there are dozens more: Gairloch, where the first hole is known as "Leabaidh". After the Disruption in the Church of Scotland in 1843, the lairds locked dissident Free Church ministers out of their premises. At Gairloch, they preached their sermons out of doors, at Leabaidh, Gaelic for "a bed". Other splendid courses include Golspie Golf Course, another links affair designed by James Baird; Reay Golf Club in north Caithness undoubtedly contains unexcavated Neolithic settlements buried in its sand dunes; Helmsdale, Bonar Bridge and Tain all have excellent courses.

North over the turbulent waves of the Pentland Firth, beyond the red-scarred cliffs of the Island of Hoy, there are splendid courses in Stromness and Kirkwall in Orkney and the most northerly golf course in the UK, at Burrafirth on the Island of Unst in Shetland. But my most enduring memory of playing golf in Scotland is of the course at Askernish, near the birthplace of Flora MacDonald on the Island of South Uist in the Outer Hebrides. It was in June. The fertile machair lands were at their finest, a fifty-kilometre-long riot of glorious multicoloured wildflowers. The clubhouse, a broken-down hut, was closed but visitors were invited to leave their green fee in "the box provided". It was hard to do so, the box in question being otherwise engaged rearing a family of starlings. The course is being "modernised" but is still wild and beautiful. Come along and find the magic of the outstanding golf courses in the glorious Northlands of Scotland.

Further Information: Highland Golf, *published by The Northern Times Ltd, Sutherland Press House, Golspie, Sutherland, Scotland KW10 6RA; Tel: 01408 633993.*

15.
The Silver Tay

We slept in the heather beneath an ink-black, star-bright sky. A velvet cloud of pipistrelle bats whisked out into the darkness from ruined croft buildings. A fox barked sharply in the distance. A solemn owl ghosted by on silent wings. Late curlew called hauntingly. Loch water lapped the shores of my dreams and sleep came easy in that warm night.

This resting-place was on the margins of Loch Ordie in Perthshire, high above the River Tay near the cathedral City of Dunkeld. Our Boy Scout camp was based on the banks of the river at Inver Park and we had set out earlier that morning on an adventure hike into the wilderness crags of Deuchary Hill (240m). In these few hours, I fell hopelessly in love with the River Tay.

From its source in the west amongst the thread-fingered busy streams of Ben Lui (1,130m) by Tyndrum, to the vast expanse of the Firth of Tay, the river runs 193 kilometres. It draws strength from an area of more than 7,300 square kilometres. Waters from the mountains of Breadalbane and Glen Lednock feed mighty Loch Tay. They flow from the ribbon of lochs of Laidon, Rannoch and Tummel, and from autumn-purple Forest of Atholl tributaries and mingle in the sea-salt tide by the fair City of Perth.

The constant Tay encapsulates Scotland's story. Neolithic man has left his mark in stone circles near Killin, and at Dowally four miles north from Dunkeld. There is evidence of 4,000-year-old homesteads in the lands of Strathtummel, Strathardle and Glenshee. Crannogs, defensive homes built on natural or artificially created islands, edged Loch Tay. A crannog reconstruction may be seen at the east end of the loch near Kenmore.

In AD 85, the Romans built fortifications at Inchtuthil, north from

Perth. Apart from unsuccessful attempts to subdue the natives, they indulged in pearl fishing. Scottish pearls were highly prized by the glitterati back in Rome.

Dunkeld Cathedral's links with Christianity go back as far as the sixth century when Celtic monks from Iona established a settlement on the banks of the Tay. St Columba is thought to have visited Dunkeld during his missionary work amongst the Picts. In AD 884, King Kenneth MacAlpine chose Dunkeld as one of the capital cities of his newfound kingdom, the other being Scone near Perth.

During the Scottish Wars of Independence, Clan MacDougall won a victory over Robert Bruce at Dalrigh in the hills above Killin at the west end of Loch Tay. The Clan possesses a magnificent brooch, torn from the plaid of the fleeing King of Scots.

James V hunted in Glen Tilt, where the River Tilt hurries to join the River Garry, a once important tributary of the Tay, now sadly robbed of most of its water to service hydro-electric power generation. In 1529, the Earl of Atholl built a hunting lodge there for King James V when 1,000 men were employed to herd deer down from the corries of Beinn a'Ghlo for His Majesty's pleasure. His daughter, Mary, Queen of Scots, was similarly entertained in Glen Tilt in 1564, before she became the hunted one.

The most famous "hunted" ones of the Tay are, however, its Atlantic salmon. The Tay is the pre-eminent European salmon fishery. For hundreds of years, *Salmo salar* has provided sustenance and sport for local fishermen and visitors alike. John Richardson described the Tay salmon fishings thus in 1788: "The fishings employ between two and three hundred fishers. Six vessels are employed during the season running to and from London which is the principal market. A considerable part are sent fresh in the spring season, and for the past two years, the greatest proportion of the fresh salmon has been packed in ice."

In 1969, 104,492 salmon were caught in the Tay District alone. Sadly, today, because of the sheer greed and stupidity of regulators and river owners, the total number of salmon caught in the whole of Scotland has sunk to less than 50,000. Indeed, many distinct populations of fish may now face extinction. Great efforts are being made to reverse the decline, but whether or not it will be in time to save Scotland's salmon remains to be seen.

Salmon were abundant in 1922 when Miss Georgina Ballantine – fishing with her father, who had rented the fishing from the Laird of Glendelvine, Sir Alexander Lyle – landed Scotland's heaviest rod-and-line caught salmon, a fish weighing 64lbs. It was displayed in the window of PD Malloch's shop in Perth. Georgina listened to two elderly men as they marvelled at the great fish. She said later, "One said to the other, 'A woman? Nae woman ever took a fish like that oot of the water, mon. I would need a horse, a block and tackle, tae tak a fish like that oot. A woman – that's a lee [lie] anyway.' I had a quiet chuckle up my sleeve and ran to catch the bus."

The Tay has always been famous for the quality and size of its salmon, and more than twenty fish of over 50lbs in weight have been taken from the river. A salmon of 71lbs was recorded as being hooked and played, but not landed, in 1868 by Dr Browne, Bishop of Bristol. He was fishing near the mouth of the River Earn, a tributary of the Tay that flows into the Firth of Tay from the south. After a battle lasting ten hours, the fish broke free.

The closest I have come to Tay salmon happened near the end of our Boy Scout camping trip. We had built a raft, and a friend and I thought that we would give it a "Viking" send off: floating down stream on it, and then diving off and leaving it to its fate before reaching the point where Thomas Telford's graceful bridge spans the Tay. The river, seventy-five yards wide at that point, was high after rain and we soon realised our folly as the strong current gripped us. It was impossible to paddle to the bank. We dived in and struck out for the shore.

I immediately felt a stomach-churning pang of panic as the flood hit me. I swam hard, vividly aware of the approaching rapids below the bridge. I made the bank just above the bridge, 300 yards down the river from where I had dived in. My companion joined me a moment later. Glad to be alive, we climbed the steps up onto the bridge and hiked shamefaced and embarrassed back to camp in our swimming trunks.

In earlier times, the bridge caused embarrassment of a different kind to its owner, the Duke of Atholl. The Duke built the bridge in 1809 and for seventy years charged a toll for crossing. Dunkeld people had to pay to meet trains in Birnam, across the river, and Birnam people paid to go to church in Dunkeld. Either way, the laird won. Locals meekly coughed up for half a century before complaining. When riots broke out in 1856, the military were called in to quell them but, even so, it was not until 1879 that the Duke was persuaded by the County Council to give up his rights.

Dunkeld is a perfect centre for exploring the Tay and its tributaries and the scent of evening woodsmoke drifting above the clustered houses is one of my enduring memories. The surrounding woodlands are quite magnificent: beech, oak, sycamore, birch, ash, pine and fir. A Douglas fir of more than thirty metres in height, by the banks of the River Braan on a walk to view a glorious waterfall, is said to be the tallest tree in Britain.

One night, whilst walking in the woods above Birnam, I surprised a capercaillie, the Gaelic "great cock of the wood". This magnificent bird was hunted to extinction in Scotland by the mid-seventeenth century. The Campbell Earls of Breadalbane reintroduced it in 1837 at Drummond Hill, which overlooks the north shore of Loch Tay at Kenmore.

Another object of great size may be viewed from Drummond Hill: the dark, blue-grey bulk of Taymouth Castle on the banks of the river. The castle was enlarged extensively by Breadalbane lairds over the years and visited by Queen Victoria in 1842. It is reported that she was pleased by her reception, commenting that it was "princely and romantic". Hundreds of Breadalbane's tenants were employed to build and light fires on the surrounding hills for the entertainment of the diminutive Queen.

When the grey finger of dawn inched its way into my sleeping bag, I awoke to find mist shimmering over the calm waters of Loch Ordie. Around me in the heather lay my companions, one by one stirring to greet the coming day. We cluttered about, washing in the loch, making breakfast. It was sad to leave, to tramp back down the hill to civilisation. But as we cleared the lower forest, like a silver thread, the River Tay lay before me and I felt as though I had returned home.

Further information about the River Tay and Perthshire may be obtained from the Perthshire Tourist Board, Lower City Mills, West Mill Street, Perth PH1 5QP, Scotland; Tel: 01738 450600; Email: perth@visitscotland.com

16.
George Heriot, the Royal Banker, Goldsmith and Jeweller

As the sun rose over Edinburgh on Wednesday, 19 June 1566, the town's goldsmiths brushed sleep from their eyes, breakfasted on porridge, haddock and oatcakes and set off for their kraams – wooden workshops built against the walls of St Giles Kirk.

In the kraams, apprentice goldsmiths tended their Master's furnace fires whilst nearby the wool and linen merchants of the Lawnmarket prepared for their weekly sale. Across the street from St Giles, the stench of rotting fish and poultry innards emanating from Fishmarket Close filled the air.

Picking his way carefully through the littered wynds, master goldsmith George Heriot greeted two colleagues, James Mossman and James Cok. All three wore the uniform of their profession, scarlet coat and black cocked hat. Each carried a gold-tipped stick. One topic dominated their conversation: the birth that morning of a son to Mary, Queen of Scots.

As the day lengthened, servants cleaned dusty rooms, laid fires and emptied their masters' chamber pots onto the streets where barefoot children begged for food and played amidst the middens. Bonfires were lit and the great and good gathered in St Giles to pray for the royal child.

Heriot lived in the High Street amidst the tall buildings that crowded either side of the "Royal Mile" from Holyrood Palace to the castle. Paved with stone, the street was narrow in its beginnings. However, from the Netherbow, the gateway to the city, the buildings were tightly packed; a maze of dark passageways constricted by the city's defensive Flodden Wall; a warren of humanity embracing 7,500 souls.

When Mary's son, James, became King of Scotland on the enforced abdication of his mother, the country divided into two factions: those who supported the Queen and those who supported the King. But in May 1573, Mary's hopes of restoration ended when Edinburgh Castle fell to the King's Party.

The town hangman, the "Doomster", was busy. He lived in Fishmarket Close near to the Tolbooth where executions were carried out. Nick-named "The Magpie" for his black silver-laced coat, he "attended" to Kirkcaldy of Grange, who had held the castle for the Queen's Party. Grange was hung and dismembered and his head spiked on the Castle wall. Next followed Heriot's friends and fellow goldsmiths, James Mossman and James Cok. Their "crime" was minting coins for the Queen's Party.

By European standards, sixteenth-century Scotland was impoverished. Gold and silver was most noticeable by its scarcity. But during Mary's reign, and both before and after her sad tenure of the Scottish Crown, Scotland was remarkable for the beauty of its coinage.

The goldsmiths guild that produced these pieces had authority to search out and destroy the work of anyone who was not a Master Goldsmith. After an apprenticeship of seven years, those who wished to become masters had to make "ane sufficient assay, pruiform try of all his cunnyng and experience in baith workmanship and knowledge of the fyenes of the metils".

Some test pieces may still be seen today. In 1586, John Mossman made the Roseneath Communion Cup, a slender bowl above a simple spreading foot, now in Huntley House Museum in the Canongate. But the most famous is "The Heriot Loving Cup" – "a Nautilus shell with silver mounts, set on a slender stem spreading into a stepped, chased foot".

The cup is erroneously named because Robert Denniestoun in fact made it. George Heriot (Snr) only supervised its production. The "Loving Cup" is owned by the famous Edinburgh school named in honour of Heriot's son, also George, who left the bulk of his fortune to establish a hospital and school "for the maintenance relief and bringing up and education of poor fatherless bairns, freemen sons of Edinburgh".

William Wallace, Master Mason, and his successor, William Aytoun, supervised the building of the school and work was completed in June 1659. That caustic commentator on all things Scottish, the Welshman Thomas Pennant, visiting Scotland in 1771, said: "Heriot's hospital is a fine old building, much too magnificent for the end proposed, that of educating poor children."

As James VI asserted his authority, the rising financial star in the crowded town was Heriot's son. He followed his father into the Goldsmiths Guild, married and set up in business on his own account and father Heriot lived to see his son rise to the peak of his profession.

Heriot was appointed goldsmith to Queen Anne in 1597. Four years later, he was appointed jeweller to the King. Such was the volume of business he conducted with the royal family that private rooms were made available to him in Holyrood Palace. Heriot was in effect the Royal Banker and became known as "jingling Geordie" because of the sound of gold coins rattling in his pockets.

The permanence of the established order that sustained Heriot ended on the evening of 26 March 1603. Sir Robert Carey cantered through the gates of Holyrood Palace bringing momentous news from London. He was ushered into the King's presence: "The Queen is dead, Your Majestie is King of England."

James had instructed Heriot to follow him to London but in the midst of this triumph, Heriot's wife Christian died. Shortly afterwards, his two sons, sailing from Leith to join their father, were drowned when their vessel foundered in a storm.

Nevertheless, Heriot prospered mightily in London, buying and selling jewellery on the Queen's behalf, making new pieces for her and for her friends, lending money whenever Anne needed it. The King also made frequent recourse to Heriot's services, as did his immediate circle and Heriot decided it was time to set aside grief and remarry.

He travelled to Edinburgh to seek a wife, the lady in question being a daughter of James Primrose, Clerk to the Privy Council. Heriot was forty-five, his bride, Alison, sixteen. The couple married in the autumn of 1608.

When Heriot returned to London, he realised he needed more staff.

Because of his special relationship with the King and Queen, Heriot made sure he employed only the best. In March 1609, a proclamation was issued requiring every magistrate in the Kingdom to recommend suitable tradesmen for the Royal Jeweller.

Whilst Queen Anne remained Heriot's most important customer, her debts, amounting to some £20,000, had become scandalous. It required a delicate touch to raise the matter with the King. James was incensed but had little option other than to pay up and hope to curb her future excesses.

Heriot paid his raw material suppliers in Portugal and Spain and set to work with a will, proud of his young wife and hopeful of starting a new family with her. But fate struck again: on 16 April 1612, Alison died. Heriot had a monument erected to her in St Gregory's Parish Church, now part of St Paul's Churchyard, and wrote, "She cannot be too much lamented who could not be too much loved."

His misfortune was compounded by the fact that Queen Anne was again up to her ears in debt and Heriot was the principal creditor. But James and Anne had also suffered personal loss. Young Prince Henry, heir to the crown of England and Scotland, had died. Heriot was loath to bring up the subject of the Queen's debts but his creditors were pressing.

Heriot petitioned the King: "Having served Your Majesty for the long period of twenty-four years without ever having sought or obtained any recompense for the same ..." The King's response to his banker's cry for help was less than complete. Only part of the debt was paid. But it was enough to stabilise Heriot's affairs. As for the King, he was finally rid of his profligate Queen when she died in 1619 at the age of forty-five.

Heriot had been badly shaken and considered returning to Edinburgh. In the meantime, however, he found consolation in the arms of mistresses by whom he had two daughters, both of whom he acknowledged. He lived in a fine house in St Martin's-in-the-Field and even in his declining years, retained tight control over every aspect of his business. As the end came, he began to make decisions about how the fortune he had amassed was to be used after his death.

He had no immediate heir, being childless apart from his two "love-begotten" daughters. As matters stood, his estate would pass to Franchischetta Heriot, the only child of his brother Patrick who had died in Genoa in Italy, but Heriot wanted to do more with his fortune. He decided to leave the bulk of his money to Edinburgh City Council to establish his school and hospital.

Heriot died in London on 12 February 1624 and was buried at St Martin's-in-the-Field. Sir Walter Balanquall, his nephew and Dean of Rochester, preached the sermon. Digging the grave and other funeral duties cost £7.6s 0d, the wake, £14.13s 4d. Heriot would not have begrudged these expenses: the motto of the school that bears his name is "We distribute chearfullie".

As the sun rises over Edinburgh today, boys and girls, dressed in their distinctive cobalt blue jackets, cross the High Street by St Giles Cathedral and make their way up George IV Bridge past Greyfriar's Church to George Heriot's School. Although now mainly a fee-paying school, it still cares "for the maintenance relief and bringing up and education of poor fatherless bairns, freemen sons of Edinburgh" and Heriot's legacy lives on.

17.
The City of Inverness, "Inversneckie", the Capital of the Highlands

Lady Mackintosh lived stylishly at No. 43 Church Street, Inverness, in 1745. Bonnie Prince Charlie was her guest before he and his kilted host headed south in hot pursuit of his father's lost crown. The following April, after the rout of the Jacobite army on Drumossie Moor, the victorious Duke of Cumberland also put his Hanovarian feet under Lady Mackintosh's dining room table. She said later, "I have had two king's bairns living with me in my time, and I wish I may never have another."

I first put my toes under an Inverness table as a young man when attending a Royal Highland Show there in 1955. Or it could have been 1956. I can't remember. Whatever, it was the last time the event was held in the Capital of the Highlands – "Inversneckie" to its friends – prior to finding a permanent home at Ingliston on the outskirts of Auld Reekie. This was my introduction to the north and I loved it, particularly the grace and charm of the old town on the banks of the fast-flowing River Ness.

Today, Inverness has been elevated to the status of City, the first Scottish town to be granted such honour in more than 100 years. The douce inhabitants greeted this achievement with their customary reserve but Provost Bill Smith said: "To be granted city status from the Queen is a magnificent honour for Inverness and will give businesses in the town and throughout the Highlands a tremendous marketing tool in attracting additional income to our fast-growing economy."

Clan Sandison has played a significant role in promoting that "economy". For a quarter of a century, Inverness has been our principal shopping centre.

A function it performs superbly. Given the choice of stumbling about Princes Street in Edinburgh or Sauchiehall Street in Glasgow, Inverness wins hands down, every time. It has all the facilities and range of choice to be found in a major city with none of the attendant hassle. We live 100 miles north from Inverness in the small township of Tongue and do not begrudge the journey. It is time and money well spent.

The population of Inverness has doubled over the past twenty years and is now more than 40,000. At the time of the Jacobite Rebellion, however, it was little more than 3,000. Four principal streets of a few hundred houses clustered around the Mercat Cross and the Town House. Then, as now, Inverness was the most important town in the north of Scotland. Most of the great Highland Clan Chiefs owned a house in Inverness and all business, trade and commerce was conducted at the Mercat Cross.

A northern "Stone of Destiny" is incorporated in the Mercat Cross: the "Clach-na-Cuddain Stone". Woman returning from the River Ness with washing or water used this stone as a resting-place. Local lore claims that so long as this famous stone remains undisturbed, so long will Inverness flourish. The original Town House, built in 1708, was the residence of Lord Lovat, who earned himself the dubious distinction of being the last man to be publicly beheaded in Britain – his reward for the part he played in Bonnie Prince Charlie's disastrous rebellion.

In the aftermath of the Battle of Culloden, the people of Inverness hastily rearranged their political sympathies and warmly greeted the government army and its fat commander, Cumberland, known to this day as "Stinking Billy". The town's jails and kirkyards were soon packed with prisoners – fit men, the wounded and the dying huddled together with little food, water or medical attention to alleviate their suffering.

The Provost of Inverness, John Fraser, and his predecessor in that office, John Hossack, petitioned General Hawley on the prisoners' behalf. The General, who had set up headquarters in the Town House, had Hossack kicked down the stairs and into the street. Fraser was ordered to clean the General's stables but allowed to pay others to do the loathsome work on his behalf. They became known as "Provost Kick" and "Provost Muck".

The oldest surviving building in Inverness is Abertarff House on Church Street, built in 1594 and now the Highland office of the National Trust for Scotland. Also in Church Street, on the walls of numbers 77–79, is a carved stone with the initials AS and HP, separated by a heart and commemorating a marriage in the Schives family. The practice of erecting "marriage lintels" was commonplace in seventeenth century Scotland. Nearby Bow Court, dating from 1720, was attractively restored in 1972 and is now home to a splendid group of flats and shops.

Inverness, ancient and modern, is ideal for a Highland adventure. Within a thirty-mile drive from the centre of town, hill walkers and climbers will find more than enough to keep them fully energised. Local golf courses are of world-class standard. There is excellent game fishing for salmon, trout and sea-trout. Indeed, Inverness is one of the few cities I know where you are likely to meet a fully kitted-out angler, complete with waders, landing net and fishing rod, strolling unconcernedly and unremarked down the High Street to do business in the River Ness.

One summer afternoon, I was walking by the river near Inverness Cathedral when an excited visitor grabbed me by the arm. "Look, Look!" he exclaimed, pointing to the middle of the stream. "It's the Loch Ness Monster!" He was almost correct. The fish was a monster but going to Loch Ness, not from it. A huge salmon was surging upstream, its vast back out of the water. I estimated the weight of the fish to have been at least 40lbs, if not more. As we anglers say, it would have been "worth the hauding", which means worth hooking, playing and landing.

Inverness Castle dominates the city and river. It is perched on a grassy hillock in the centre of town. The present red sandstone structure was built between 1834 and 1846 but it stands on the remains of much older fortifications, variously bashed about a bit by successive waves of less than friendly visitors – the last being Bonnie Prince Charlie's army, who blew up the castle to prevent it being used by their enemies. A graceful monument to one of my most-loved Scottish heroines, Flora MacDonald, guards the front door.

After helping Prince Charles to escape, Flora was incarcerated in the Tower of London. The Duke of Cumberland visited her there to ask why she had assisted his father's enemy. Flora is said to have responded that she would have done the same for any man in such a position, regardless of politics or religion. The statue is inscribed with the comment Samuel Johnson made when he met Flora during his tour of the Highlands: "The preserver of Prince Charles Edward Stuart will be mentioned in history and if courage and fidelity be virtues, mentioned with honour."

One man who knows the nooks and crannies of Inversneckie better than most has the same Macdonald surname and similar lineage: the late John Macdonald, editor of the *Inverness Courier*, whose crofting ancestors lived for generations on the Island of Skye. The *Inverness Courier* celebrated its 175th year of publication in November 1992 and is required reading throughout the north. I asked John what he thought about his town's grand new status. "Well," he replied laconically, "if it doesn't do you any good it won't do you any harm."

John Macdonald believes passionately that Inverness is "as near perfect an urban community as any place can be". An exile for much of his journalistic life, working with the *British Reader's Digest*, *Daily Telegraph* and *The Times*, John is also an authority on the American Civil War. His book, *Great Battles of the Civil War*, published by Michael Joseph in 1989, was greeted with wide critical acclaim and is a definitive work on the subject. He told me when he last visited Gettysburg, walking up the Confederate lines and down the Union lines, a visitor driving a car stopped him.

"What are you doing?" the man asked.

John told him he was walking the lines.

"Are you mad?" came the reply. "Nobody walks!"

Walking is the best way to discover the heart and soul of the "Capital of the Highlands" and there are seven bridges over the river to help you do so. There is enduring pleasure to be had in mingling with local people as they go about their business. Listen to their soft Scottish accent, adjudged to be the purest form of spoken English heard anywhere in the world. Listen to the sound of the old stream hurrying by to greet the cold waters of the Moray Firth. Look over the River Ness to the fourteenth-century Parish Church of St Mary. Say a silent prayer for the Jacobite prisoners who suffered and died there for Bonnie Prince Charlie so long ago.

Further information from: Inverness Tourist Centre, Castle Wynd, Inverness IV2 3BJ; Tel: 01463 234353; Fax: 01463 710609.

18.
Dornoch

~~~~~

On a mild autumn morning I wandered amongst the grey tombstones surrounding Dornoch Cathedral in east Sutherland. The dew-wet sparkling grass bore the imprint of my passing footsteps. Jet-black jackdaws croaked from the cockerel-capped weather vane above the tower. Collared doves cooed on the branches of ancient trees nodding round the quiet city square. The sense of peace was palpable.

There are grander cathedrals than Dornoch, more awe-inspiring buildings more magnificently designed and decorated, but I know of no other cathedral that so immediately captivates the spirit. A contract has been struck here between man and his maker, a happy union that neither intimidates nor demands obsessive obedience. The old sandstone structure exudes life and love.

The Royal Burgh of Dornoch has been the religious and administrative centre of Sutherland for more than 800 years. Today, the busy A9 Inverness/ Thurso road bypasses it and this may be the reason why this small community on the shores of the sea-blue firth has retained its unique character. The next time you pass this way, visit Dornoch. Your only problem will be in leaving it.

You will be following famous names when you do so, particularly names of people afflicted with golf: Nick Faldo, Greg Norman, Tom Watson, Bob Charles, Andy North and Chip Black, all of whom have extolled the excellence of world-famous Royal Dornoch Golf Course. Earlier visitors included Tom Morris, Harry Vardon, Bobby Locke, Bobby Jones and Bing Crosby.

Old Tom Morris from St Andrews designed the course and he greatly influenced two Dornoch men, Donald Ross and his brother Alec. Donald went on to become one of the most famous course designers in the history of the game. He and his brother immigrated to America at the end of the nineteenth century where Donald designed more than 500 courses, including Pinehurst No. 2 course and the Seminole Course in Florida.

Multi-millionaire and philanthropist Andrew Carnegie had a "holiday cottage" nearby at Skibo Castle and he and his wife, Louise, were introduced to the Royal and Ancient game at Dornoch. The magnate presented the Carnegie Shield to the Royal Dornoch Golf Club and it is said to be "one of the most beautiful golf trophies in the world". The Shield is on display in the clubhouse.

Golf and Dornoch are inseparable. People have been playing Scotland's national game on the links here for more than 400 years. The course was laid out in 1616, although it is more likely than not that the clerics of Dornoch disported themselves thus well before that time. After all, monks from St Andrews, the home of golf, were "posted" to Dornoch and I'll bet they lugged their clubs along with them.

The religious importance of Dornoch reaches even further back in time. By AD 1140, a cell of Benedictine monks from Dunfermline had established themselves in Dornoch, when King David I, "for the love of him", asked the Earl of Orkney and Caithness to protect the monks from injury and shame.

That they needed such protection was beyond doubt. Two previous Bishops had come to a grisly end in Caithness: Bishop John was mutilated and murdered at Scrabster in 1202 and Bishop Adam met a similar fate in Halkirk in 1222. The seat of the Bishopric was thus moved south to the relative safety of Dornoch and in 1224, Bishop Gilbert, the newly appointed Bishop of Caithness, began his great work of founding the cathedral.

Looking out over the well-tended golf links and fertile fields round Dornoch, it is hard to think of these lands as being once an embattled "frontier". The truth is that hardly an inch of soil in this corner of Sutherland is unstained with the blood of some feud or bitter battle. I went in search of the burial place of one of the participants, the Norseman Earl Sigurd the Mighty, who was killed during a fearsome scrap in about AD 900.

Norse domination of the firthlands of Ross and Sutherland was a constant thorn in the flesh of burgeoning Scottish nationhood. According to the *Orkneyinga Saga*, Sigurd was slain by a local earl named Máel Brigte. As was the custom, Máel Brigte cut off his opponent's head and slung it over the saddle of the horse he was riding. In doing so, however, his leg was scratched by one of the unfortunate Sigurd's teeth and this wound caused Máel Brigte's death shortly afterwards.

I drove south west from Dornoch, bordering the calm waters of the firth, to find Cyderhall Farm and the mound under which the Viking warrior lies. Five fine sycamore trees greeted me, a flock of sheep and lambs baa-ing urgently under their leafy branches. The mound is to the left of a farm track on a small hillock, Cnoc Skardie, near the slow-flowing Evelix River. Well, he is reputed to be there. Not having a spade or shovel with me at the time, I can't confirm this truth. But I swear I heard him cough.

Back in Dornoch, I called at the Dornoch Castle Hotel, across the road from the cathedral. This remarkable building was formerly the Bishop's palace and it retains much of its early character. At the foot of a tall semi-circular tower there is a small doorway. A winding stone staircase leads to the reception area on the first floor. The bar is half-panelled in dark wood and there is a huge stone fireplace where the scent of burning peat lingers. Stag's heads glower from the walls below a timbered ceiling.

The walled garden, overlooked by a stone balustrade balcony, is a "secret" garden, almost not of this world in its calm beauty. Stately Yew trees form an avenue, centred by a green verdigris-stained statue on a plinth of the Greek God Pan, busy piping. Inscribed around the base is the name Beatrice Sykes, whose home the castle was before it became a hotel.

The castle, cathedral and town were less peaceful when "visited" by rapacious Caithness and Strathnaver neighbours in 1570. The then Earl of Caithness, George, was determined to annex Sutherland to his lands, by fair means or foul, and he besieged Dornoch to achieve his evil ambitions. His son John, Master of Caithness, was anxious to avoid bloodshed and negotiated the handing over of hostages as a guarantee of Dornoch's future good behaviour.

Earl George was made of sterner stuff. He accepted the hostages, murdered them and then ordered the town to be burned. Much of the cathedral was destroyed, including the entire roof, and it was not until 1616 that the task of rebuilding and repairing was begun by Sir Robert Gordon; continued by Elizabeth, Duchess-Countess of Sutherland, from 1835 to 1837 and the Rev. Charles Bentinck in 1924.

I stood by the tomb of Countess Elizabeth near the communion table in the Chancel of the restored cathedral and pondered these matters. The Countess and her husband, the Duke of Stafford, were the architects of the infamous Sutherland Clearances, when they brutally evicted 16,000 of their tenants to make way for more profitable sheep. No mention of that here. Instead, on the marble slab, the words: "Her attachments to Sutherland and her clansmen were shared by her husband . . . she enjoyed the admiration and love of her family and friends."

I remembered the story of one poor woman, evicted twice during the clearances. When she eventually died, she was buried in Dornoch churchyard. Her relatives said, "Well, the Countess will move you no more, now." Remarkably, the Countess did. The restoration work she began required a number of graves to be "relocated", one being the grave of the unfortunate woman who had been so persecuted.

Another poor, persecuted woman is commemorated by a rounded stone, about 2ft 6in in height, that stands in the garden of the last house in Carnaig Street. It took me a bit to find because there is no signpost to it. The Witches Stone marks the place where Janet Horne was burned in 1722 after being found guilty of witchcraft, the last such judicial execution to be carried out in Scotland.

I left the Witches Stone and drove out to Dornoch Airfield – a grass field with a wind-sock and a wooden shack at one end. The shack was locked and the only sign of business was a notice on the yellow painted door asking aviators to pop flight details in a red letter box. I walked from the terminal building across the saltmarsh dunes between the golf practice area and the sea.

This is a wildlife paradise, alive with the cry of curlew and red-billed oyster-catcher, decked with wildflowers: yellow rattle, grass of parnassus, marsh orchid, frog orchid, mouse-ear hawksweed, Baltic rush and ragged robin, some of which are rare in Scotland. From the dunes, I looked down onto a vast crescent of spotless golden sands that stretched north as far as the white-painted edifice of Dunrobin Castle near Golspie.

Before leaving, I returned to the cathedral to make my farewells to Bishop Gilbert. Afternoon sunlight slanted in through the splendid stained-glass windows and splashed at my feet. I said a prayer for all those who had laboured so hard to preserve this glorious building which so enhances our understanding of the importance of humility in modern times. And to ask for some help also in burnishing up my entirely hopeless golf swing.

For further details, contact: Tourist Information Centre, The Square, Dornoch, Sutherland IV25 3SD. Tel: 01862 810400.

19.
Discovering Shetland

The Shetland Island accent makes music out of words. When Ann and I were there in June 2009, a friend gave us a copy of *The Shetland Dictionary*, inscribed, "Aa du needs ta ken aboot kabes and humlibands." Meaning, "All you need to know about how to row Shetland boats." Ann and I are anglers. Shetland people are proud of their pristine environment and work hard to keep it that way. For instance, visitors are advised, "Dunna chuck bruck," don't scatter litter.

My ancestors come from Shetland and the islanders are an independent race. I remember discussing the question of Home Rule for Scotland with a friend in Lerwick, the largest town in Shetland. He was less than impressed. "It would make little difference to us, Bruce," he said, "being ruled from Edinburgh or from London. The one would be just as bad as the other." Indeed, Lerwick is nearer to Bergen in Norway than it is to Edinburgh, Scotland's capital city.

Shetland comprises 100 islands covering an area of more than 1,295 square kilometres. The principal isles are Mainland, Bressay, Whalsay, Fetlar, Yell and Unst. From AD 875 until 1468, they belonged to Norway. Then they were pledged to Scotland as part of the dowry when King James III married Margaret, daughter of King Christian I of Norway. This Norse influence is still evident in the characteristic design of Shetland boats, the domestic architecture and in Shetland place names.

There is no "best" time to visit these magical northern isles. They lie beyond Orkney, 110 miles north from mainland Scotland, and are always welcoming. Their overwhelming beauty instantly ensnares the soul. But June is a captivating month. As the islands awaken from the grip of winter to embrace summer, midnight is as bright as dawn during the long twilight of Shetland evenings, the "simmer dim". This is the ideal moment to launch a boat and fish for your supper on Shetland trout lochs.

The largest freshwater loch is Loch of Spiggie, near Sumburgh Airport on South Mainland. It is owned by the Royal Society for the Protection of Birds and is an important nature reserve. We had a wonderful evening's trout fishing there, serenaded by curlew and whimbrel. On the west shore, by Littleness, in times past, non-anglers used to splash and splutter in Hallelujah Bay – adherents of the Baptist faith were "ducked" there into membership of their church.

We stayed near Ocraquoy, a few miles south from Lerwick. There were splendid walks from our front door and we rarely needed the car. One morning, we tramped north to Coall Head (64m). At Bay of Ocraquoy, we were greeted by a symphony orchestra of be-whiskered barking seals, eyeing us cautiously, paralleling our passage along the shore.

A headland was decked overall in a carpet of blue squill. Yellow flag nodded by tiny ochre-coloured burns. In one small corner we found more squill, along with tormentil, marsh orchid, spotted orchid, lousewort, lesser celandine, white and lilac cuckoo flower, sorrel, red campion, sea rocket, silverweed and milkwort all growing together in happy unison. We beach-combed Bay of Fladdabister and climbed to the ruins of old limekilns, still in use in the 1930s, to have lunch. They made the perfect dining room: grass-lined hollows, sheltered from the wind with a place to rest tired backs. Sea sound and gull cry eased our spirits.

Lerwick is the bustling commercial centre of Shetland. The harbour is invariably packed with ships of all nations. During our visit, we watched the arrival of the graceful sailing boats taking part in the Bergen to Shetland race. The main street is flagstone-paved and many houses have direct access to the sea. A replica of a Viking longship, the *Dim Riv*, rides at anchor and during summer months, visitors can enjoy trips round the bay with a difference: they have to row the boat themselves. On one occasion, two less-than-experienced American lady oarswomen came ashore after never once having managed to get their oars into the water, but delighted nevertheless with the experience.

Other unforgettable visitor experiences are the ancient monuments that abound in Shetland. Just outside Lerwick is a settlement site and broch on Loch of Clickimin, occupied from 700 BC to the fifth or sixth century AD. Close to Loch of Spiggie is Jarlshof, a settlement that was used by successive cultures for 3,000 years. On Mousa Island, off the east coast of South Mainland, is Europe's best preserved broch, built around the time of the birth of Christ. By the Loch of Asta, close to the first tee of a delightful little 9-hole golf course, there is a 4,000-year-old Neolithic standing stone. Touch these ancient stones. Listen. Hear the sound of children laughing. Smell peat smoke rising from cooking fires.

During our Shetland sojourn we paid our respects to Shetland's old "capital", Scalloway, on the west coast. The town is dominated by the gaunt ruins of Scalloway Castle, built by Earl Patrick Stewart, a monster, renowned for his brutality. Dinner with Patrick, if he became angry, could be a dangerous affair. We found nearby Scalloway College restaurant much more user-friendly and a must when you are in Shetland. They serve the finest seafood imaginable in an informal, relaxed atmosphere. Shetland wool garments are also enticing, vibrant with natural colours and remarkably inexpensive. Shetland sheep are not clipped; the wool is gently pulled out by hand.

Another must is a visit to Ireland, a cluster of houses overlooking St Ninian's Isle south from Scalloway. We arrived on a sparkling morning with the distant island of Foula clearly visible on the horizon. The sheer cliffs guarding Foula are 366m in height and the Vikings called the island *Flugloy*, "The Island of the Birds". On the shore of Ireland Wick ("wick" is the Norse name for a bay) lay a classic Shetland-style boat, pointed at both ends, broad-beamed and utterly beautiful. They say in Shetland that you may do as you please with another man's wife but you must never lay hands on his boat. Nobody was looking, so I risked stroking the vessel.

St Ninian's Isle is joined to the mainland by a 656-yard-long golden sandbank. A church, dedicated to St Ninian, was built on the island in the sixth or seventh century, but the island is most famous for a hoard of treasure found in 1958. A fifteen-year-old schoolboy, Douglas Coutts, who had volunteered to help excavate the site, made the find. Douglas recalled the moment: "I got down to a stone slab marked with a Celtic cross. Beneath this stone was a box, which contained the collection of silverware which has been dated back to 800 AD. The cache included twelve brooches of Celtic design, many inset with semi-precious stones, numerous bowls and a hanging lamp and other objects."

On the island of Yell, a bumpy boat ride across a narrow stretch of sea appropriately named the "buttocks", we parked by the ruins of Windhouse, which is haunted by a family of ghosts: the Lady in Silk, whose broken-necked skeleton was discovered under floorboards at the foot of the staircase; the Man in Black, a tall spectre, dressed in a black cloak and noted for his ability to walk through walls; the Child, whose remains were found built into the kitchen wall; and a black dog to keep them company.

Nobody was home when we called, so we tramped out to explore the deserted village of Vollister. A track leads north from Windhouse above Whale Firth, crossing Brocken Burn on the slopes of Muckle Swart Houll (110m). After about a mile, you will see the ruins of the village ahead on a promontory overlooking the firth. Vollister was cleared of its people in the latter years of the nineteenth century. All that remains to mark their passing are broken buildings and a rusty boat-mooring ring in a rock by the shore.

Further north, on the Island of Unst, another ghost is commemorated in the name of ale brewed in Scotland's most northerly brewery, the Valhalla Brewery at Baltasound. It is called "White Wife". This woman appears in cars, generally being driven by lone men. She was last seen by Steven Spence in 1996 whilst he was driving along the road two miles south from Baltasound. The ale is pretty stunning, too – dry and refreshing, bitter with a characteristically fruity after-taste.

Unst has "the most northerly" everything in UK: golf course, rugby ground, post office, castle (Muness), church and, of course, the famous lighthouse of Muckle Flugga. The lighthouse was built in 1858 by Thomas

Stevenson. As a young man, his son, the author Robert Louis Stevenson, stayed on the island. He is said to have based the shape of the island in his famous adventure story, *Treasure Island*, on the shape of Unst.

More tangible treasure has been accrued in Shetland by wise investment of the revenue gathered from the oil industry, which arrived in Shetland during the 1970s. The value of these funds has now reached £705 million, making Shetland the richest local authority in Britain. The money currently equates to a tidy £30,653 for each of the islands' 23,000 inhabitants. Whilst the oil-boom may have made Shetland rich, it has not altered the character of the people, or their deep commitment to and love of their sea-girt homeland. Just remember, avoid touching their kabes, humlibands or boats – and dunna chuck bruck.

For further information about Shetland, contact: Shetland Tourist Office, Market Cross, Lerwick, Shetland ZE1 0LU; Tel: 01595 693434; Fax: 01595 695807; Email: info@visitshetland.com; Website: www.visitshetland.com

For books about Shetland, contact: The Shetland Times Bookshop, 71–79 Commercial Street, Lerwick, Shetland ZE1 0AJ; Tel: 01595 695531; Fax: 01595 692897; Email: bookshop@shetland-times.co.uk; Website: http://www. shetlandtimes.co.uk/shop/

20.
Highland White Dream

Skerray is a scatter of crofts and houses clinging to the skirts of a cliff-girt headland in North Sutherland. It is pronounced "Skera". The yellow sands of Tongue Bay guard the headland to the west. In the east, Icelandic waves sweep the shores of Torrisdale Bay. The Gaelic for Skerray is "Sgeireadh" and the name means "between the rocks and seas".

Eleven crofting townships here have survived the test of time: Strathan, Modsarie, Achnabat, Skerray, Tubeg, Clashbuie, Clashaidy, Achtoty, Aird, Torrisdale and Borgie. This is the land of Clan Mackay and the predominant surname is of that ilk. At a recent children's Christmas pantomime, half of the little ones taking part in the production had the surname "Mackay". The population of Skerray – men, women and children – amounts to some eighty souls.

If you are traveling between John O'Groats and Durness in the west you can easily miss Skerray. The main road bypasses the community. To explore this magical enclave, turn right from the A836 after the stone bridge where the Borgie River tumbles seawards. A narrow, single-track route winds tortuously north to Torrisdale beach, past the tomb-stoned graveyard on the shore and through the principal townships, before rejoining highway A836 after a semi-circular journey of five miles.

But Skerray is more than just scenically magnificent. It is a thriving community, as fully engaged in the new millennium as it is proud and mindful of its Highland history and heritage. It is also a community that has successfully integrated both local and newcomer into the complex fabric of daily life. The population of Skerray is highly cosmopolitan, with a wide range of externally acquired skills mixed with local knowledge and experience.

Andrew Fraser, the Free Church minister who served his Skerray "flock" for fifteen years, puts the matter simply. He says, "The people here are amongst the most welcoming that I have ever known." Pat Rodlin, a noted horticulturist, told me: "Perhaps we get on together because we need each other. New arrivals often have little or no idea whatsoever of how to work a croft. The only way they can learn is by seeking help from those whose families have worked this land for generations."

Elizabeth "Babe" Mackay is of that line of families. She and her husband, Sinclair, live at Clashaidy, close to the harbour where Sinclair keeps his fishing boat. Babe was born in the old post office in Skerray where her father was postmaster. Babe acquired her nickname because of her childhood love of animals. Whenever one asked where she was, the response invariably was, "Oh, the babe will be up the hill with the animals."

Babe and her sisters, Catherine, Mary and Annie, followed their father's post office footsteps and the family looked after the Royal Mail in Skerray for seventy years. Babe has been a member of the Skerray Public Hall Committee ever since she left school, but she won't say exactly when that was. She is also involved in the Skerray/Borgie Community Club, Age Concern and a host of other local activities.

The present post office is in Jimson's (tel: 01641 521445), an eclectic shop in a wonderfully restored thatched croft adjacent to the most northerly garden centre on mainland Britain. Until recently, Postmistress Marilyn Macfadyen, like most other Skerray residents, played an important part in the affairs of the community. Marilyn is multitalented. She hails from Glasgow where she worked in the Scottish Civil Service. Marilyn also trained as a ballerina. She recently wrote and directed a hilarious production of *Cinderella*, performed to great acclaim before a capacity audience in the village hall. Her daughter is now the sub-postmistress.

The mainstay of horticultural activity is, however, Pat Rodlin, a native of the Orkney Islands. Pat worked extensively in Finland, Holland and Switzerland before coming to live in Skerray in 1984. She brought with her a unique chrysanthemum, the Highland White Dream, which has gained international fame and recognition. Over the past five years, approximately a quarter of a million examples of this beautiful flower have been grown at Skerray and sent all over the world.

The garden centre specialises in silver birch trees grown from locally collected seeds, as well as holly, yew, elderberry, rowan, alder, aspen and sycamore. Although the centre is small, it hosts an astonishing array of plants, all raised and cared for with loads of TLC. As well as trees, the centre has splendidly strong heather plants, alpine species, gorse and whin, all well accustomed to thriving in the harshest of climes.

Much of this enterprise is promoted through NORC-CELT (North Coast Community Enterprise Limited), set up by Skerray people to address the needs of the townships. NORC-CELT has been supported famously by funding from local government organisations as well as by generous donations from residents. Adjacent to Jimson's shop and the garden centre are the offices of "An Comann Eachdraidh Sgeireadh", the Skerray Historical Society. An absorbing archive, open to visitors, is being built up depicting the life and work of the community, based upon personal letters, documents, photographs and reminiscences.

Another mainstay of the local community is Meg Telfer, who devotes a huge amount of time and energy to promoting Skerray and its environs. But it is her work as an artist that commands most instant admiration: wide, bold, sweeping landscapes, which capture the spirit of the north far more vividly than any spoken or written words could ever hope to do. Until she retired, Meg was a visiting art teacher in local primary schools. She told me, "Teaching children art is the best job in the world."

Meg also teaches at the Skerray Studio, another string in the NORC-CELT bow. Drop-in art courses are a feature of the annual calendar where expert tuition can be arranged. All you are required to bring is enthusiasm and the desire to learn. Frances Bowman, from Skerray Mains, is also an artist. Frances specialises in watercolours. Her classes are well attended by young and not so young alike. Mike Roper runs practical courses in photography.

When Marilyn Macfadyen's production of *Cinderella* hit the Skerray boards in March, your correspondent was an unlikely Ugly Sister. His companion, affectionately known as UGS 2, was David Illingworth, a recycled teenager in his eighth decade who lives in a small cottage at Tubeg. David is a clockmaker who learned his trade during the Second World War when he worked on the Type X cypher machine, the British answer to the German Enigma encoder.

David's cottage is loud with the tick and tock of his business: fob watches, pocket-watches, wristwatches, mantel clocks, ormolu clocks, carriage clocks and longcase clocks of various sizes. The walls are adorned with his paintings, the floor with tiles designed and made by his Danish-born wife, Lotte Glob, an internationally renowned ceramicist. In spite of being eternally busy, David was, until recently, treasurer of the historical society. David says, "Living in Skerray is easy on the spirit."

Known universally as "Doc", Betty Mackenzie, a retired medical practitioner, has lived in Torrisdale for, well, quite a few years. She is a powerhouse of ideas and an active member of most of the local organisations, including being clerk to the Skerray Grazings committee who manage the communal community land. Doc's latest project is centred upon using whin and gorse chippings to prevent mice and other pests from eating prized garden plants.

She heard a report on the radio about the chippings whilst she was looking out of her window – onto a large expanse of whins: "There's a great idea, we could market gorse chippings as mulch." Wheels are already in motion and the idea is gathering speed, as do most ideas in Skerray. Doc played an important part in another highly successful Skerray idea, this time from Meg Telfer and Marilyn Macfadyen. Wool taken from individual sheep was knitted into hats, complemented with a picture of the sheep which provided the wool. Doc did the knitting.

At a time when so much is heard about depopulation and stagnant Highland communities, Skerray is an outstanding example of what can be achieved when people care about their environment and care about those who live and work in that environment. This is perhaps exemplified by a poignant plaque attached to a cattle-grid on the A836 road to the north of Skerray. It says, simply, "Willie John's Grid, 7/9/1914–13/12/1996".

Willie John Mackay was a Skerray man who fought tirelessly to have cattle-grids placed in roads to prevent wandering cattle from entering and damaging gardens. In a crofting community, traditionally, sheep and cattle are free to roam and this can sometimes cause angst and ill feeling. Finding the money to construct the grids was the problem, a problem that Willie John addressed with customary diligence. He won his battle but never lived to see the grid built. The plaque is his small memorial.

Since this piece was written, many of those featured in it have since "moved on" to the great croft in the sky. But their spirit still lives and still burns brightly in my mind and heart.

21.
Caithness Memories

Of all the airs the wind can blow, I love those from Caithness best, Scotland's Lowlands up beyond the Highlands and the home of my paternal grandfather. He was born in the fishing village of Staxigoe to the north of Wick, where his brother had a farm overlooking the cold waters of the Moray Firth. My father, John Sandison, as a young man used to spend his holidays working with his uncle and it was here that one of the most notable Caithness brawls of the 1920s was arranged. The local "Wheeper-in", the school truant officer, was also named John Sandison and had the reputation of being a useful boxer. My father was skillful in fisticuffs as well, so the town worthies determined that it would be a good idea to find out which John Sandison was the better man in the ring. The match was to be fought in a barn near Staxigoe Harbour.

A date was set and speculation on the outcome sharpened. Age and experience were on the side of the Wheeper-in but my father had the asset of youth. At the appointed hour, bales of hay were dragged into the barn to form a ring. Wagers were placed and strong drink taken. It is alleged that those who supported my father plied the Wheeper-in with copious amounts in an attempt to blur his defenses but this is pure hearsay. Stripped to the waist, the men stepped up to scratch and after half an hour of hard work, the Wheeper-in acknowledged defeat. "Lad," he said, "if I was half my age and twice as sober, it might have been a different story, but you won fair and square." They remained the best of friends.

Staxigoe is less boisterous today but it used to boast upwards of sixty vessels, bobbing in the bay: herring boats, sailing ships discharging timber from Scandinavia, the bustle of fish-curing stations on the shore – a vibrant community which lived by and from the sea. However, during the early years of the nineteenth century, Wick became the principal herring port. At its height, this fishery supported more than 1,000 boats and it is said that when they were all in port together, a man could walk dry-shod from one side of Wick Harbour to the other. The herring, "the silver darlings", made the town rich.

The small villages along the ragged coast prospered as well – Latheron, Lybster, Dunbeath and Berriedale – but perhaps the most dramatic fishing station was at Whaligoe, a few miles south from Wick. There, the harbour is situated at the base of fifty-four-metre cliffs and to reach the bottom, steps were cut into the sheer sides, descending precipitously to the sea. The catch was loaded into creels, which fishwives carried on their heads to the top of the steps to be taken from there to the gutting tubs at Wick.

After the collapse of the herring fishery, Whaligoe was deserted. However, until the 1970s, the harbour steps were cared for by Mrs Juhle, a local lady who was concerned that they may fall into disrepair. She reasoned that since Jesus had been a fisherman, then, "at the second coming", He could arrive at Whaligoe. She would make certain that the steps were in a fit state to receive Him. The steps are now cared for by the Wick Heritage Society.

The prosperity engendered by the herring fishery embraced much of the north of Scotland. As people were driven from their homes during the Highland Clearances so that the lairds could rent the land they had stolen to Lowland sheep farmers, the dispossessed trekked to Wick in search of work – men to sign on as fishermen, women and children as fish-gutters. Whole families made the journey and they followed the herring shoals down the east coast seeking employment where and when they could, then making the long journey back to the hovels that had replaced the homes out of which they had been burned by rapacious landowners.

Wick boasted the largest Gaelic-speaking congregation in the world, where 5,000 souls would gather on the Green by the Wick River to hear their ministers preach on Sunday mornings. And the ministers had plenty to say. Herring fishing was thirsty work. More than 800 gallons of whisky were drunk each week. Ministers complained bitterly that whilst it was hard to get people in for evening service, "for a wedding you could get six pipers at a stroke, and not a teetotaller amongst them".

The Wick herring industry reached its peak during the 1860s, when, due to the introduction of cotton nets, the catching capacity of the fleet vastly increased. In a few days in the 1860 season, unprecedented numbers of fish were caught: 50,160 crans containing fifty million herring. The town bustled. One man, above all, helped achieve this: James Bremner, born in the village of Keiss a few miles north from Wick.

Bremner was the most successful fish curer and an inventor of extraordinary talent. He raised 200 sunken and stranded vessels, including the world's largest steamship, Brunel's *SS Great Britain*. He designed and built sailing vessels of up to 500 tons in weight, advised Brunel on repairs to the Blackwall Tunnel under the River Thames in London when it began to leak, built more than twenty harbours, and invented a suspension crane with an expandable jib and floating work platforms.

Bremner was loved and admired by all. When he died, shops closed their shutters and window blinds were drawn. I often visit Wick Town Hall, where there is a wonderful portrait of the great man, to pay my respects, and the graceful, slim monument to him that stands on a hill on the south shore of Wick Bay overlooking the scene of so many of his labours.

Earlier rapacious visitors, the Vikings, made Caithness their home, their "Land of Cat". The Norsemen arrived toward the end of the ninth century from Orkney and tried to impress their will upon the people, not so much as invaders as settlers. But these fertile lands were also coveted by the Kings of Scotland, who were determined that they should remain in their hands and not those of the Viking Earls of Orkney. The Norse influence in Caithness ended soon after the King's bishop, Adam, was outrageously murdered. When Adam imposed a tax on butter, the tenants complained to Earl John of Orkney, who replied: "The devil take the bishop and his butter; you may roast him, if you please." Which the tenants promptly did. King Alexander II (1198–1249) was not amused and marched north to restore order.

But order was never much in evidence in Caithness during the Middle Ages. A local rhyme succinctly tells the story: "Sinclair, Keith, Sutherland and Clan Gunn, there seldom was peace where these four were in." Clan Gunn was the dominant force then, descended from Svein Asleifarson who was alive and kicking all and sundry out of his way during the twelfth century. The ruins of Svein's Caithness home may still be seen at Freswick, a few miles from the Stacks of Duncansby near John O'Groats. The site is to the south of the present fortified tower house, built by the Sinclairs of Freswick in the seventeenth century.

As Clan Gunn lost its authority and much of its land, various septs were established: the Hendersons, Williamsons and Wilsons. Other sept names included Georgeson, Jameson, Johnson, MacComas, MacCorkill, MacIan, MacKeamish, Manson, Nelson and my own bunch, Sandison. One of the most famous of the clan, Sir James Gunn, is said to have accompanied Sir Henry Sinclair, Earl of Orkney, on his voyage of discovery to the New World in 1398, almost a century before Columbus made a similar, better-known journey. Sir William Gunn, knighted by King Charles I in 1639, was a soldier of fortune who became a General and a Baron of the Holy Roman Empire. Another member of the clan named Lake Gunn in the south island of New Zealand. Perhaps the most notable, however, is Neil Gunn (1891–1973) one of Scotland's best-loved authors who was born at Dunbeath and wrote emotively about his native land in such enduring books as *The Silver Darlings* and *Highland River*.

Another important industry that was unique to Caithness was the quarrying of flagstone. In a county virtually devoid of trees, flagstone was used for fencing, for roof tiles and for floors. During the nineteenth century, when railway-building fever swept Britain, the preferred stone for platforms was Caithness flag. The Strand, in London, was paved with

Caithness flagstone and 20,000 tons were quarried each year and exported all over the world. The industry "died" with the invention of concrete, but it has revived spectacularly and Caithness flagstone is as much in demand today as it was 150 years ago.

Although quarrying is automated now, one man, the late Jack Green, still worked his quarry in the old way, by hand: raising the slabs by levers, carefully splitting and dressing the flagstones with hammer and chisel. Jack Green was still working at the age of eighty-six years and would work in his quarry from dawn to dusk. When I last called to say hello to Jack he was training up two apprentices, both men in their mid-sixties.

But the story of Caithness is as much about land as it is about people. Behind the fertile coastal fringe and the farms and fields between Wick and Thurso, lies one of the great natural wonders of the world: the Flow Country, the largest remaining example of blanket peat bog on planet Earth; a vast uninhabited area of interconnected lochs, lochans and bog pools, filled with the cry of curlew, golden plover, dunlin and greenshank; home to rare black-throated and red-throated divers, golden eagle, hen harrier, peregrine and buzzard; where red deer roam and otters play and fierce-eyed wildcat mark your passing on the purple heather moor.

This was also our family playground when we lived in Caithness. Our children learned to fish for brown trout in the Flow Country; tramped for miles with us to remote sparkling blue waters beneath cathedral skies; discovered the simple joy to be found in myriad wildflowers which grow there: bog asphodel, tormentil, wild violet, sundew, butterwort, yellow flag and red-tinged sphagnum moss. On warm summer days, we swam from silent sandy shores and, invariably, a basket of beautiful trout accompanied us home.

Caithness is a land for all seasons, as welcoming in the depths of winter as it is during the long summer nights of the "simmer dim" (summer dimness), when it never really gets dark. There are a host of things to keep you and all your tribe busy: outstanding archaeological sites such as the dramatic 4,500-year-old Neolithic burial chambers at Camster; the ruined castles of Sinclair and Girnigoe, still the official residence of the Earl of Caithness; gaunt Ackergill Tower, where Oliver Cromwell's officers were billeted during the terrible religious wars of the seventeenth century.

There are splendid links golf courses; salmon and trout fishing of angling dreams; empty golden sand beaches at Dunnet in the north and Sinclair Bay to the east; and the delights of downtown Wick and Thurso, where you will meet the kindest people in the world. However, if you're ever invited into a boxing ring up here, just remember the fate of the Wheeper-in and abjure the consumption of too much *uisge beatha*, the Water of Life.

22.
Edinburgh, "Auld Reekie"

I was born in Edinburgh and wear the old grey city like a warm blanket round my soul. I discovered the worth of the nation I love whilst growing up in "Auld Reekie"; in the closes and wynds of the Royal Mile; on monument-bedecked Calton Hill and proud Princes Street; in the calm of Holyrood Park and amidst the ancient woodlands of Cramond.

Edinburgh is above all a city of culture, and I was delighted when the United Nations Educational, Scientific and Cultural Organization (UNESCO) embraced this view. Meeting in Paris, France, in 2004, UN chiefs announced that the Scottish capital would become the world's first "City of Literature".

In the 1760s, an English visitor, John Amyat, the King's Chemist, famously declared: "Here I stand at what is called the Cross of Edinburgh, and can, in a few minutes, take fifty men of genius by the hand." This was the high point of what has become known as "The Enlightenment", when Edinburgh was the world centre of inspired thought.

These men of genius included the poet Allan Ramsay, "The Gentle Shepherd"; his son, also Allan Ramsay, portrait painter to George III; David Hume, philosopher and historian; Alexander "Jupiter" Carlyle, minister and political pamphleteer; the Reverend John Home, whose play, *Douglas*, outraged his fellow clergymen and inspired a member of the audience to call out: "Whaur's yer Wullie Shakspeare noo!"; the great architect, Robert Adam; Adam Smith, political economist and author of *The Wealth of Nations*, and many more.

The spirits of these men haunt Auld Reekie. When I walk down the Royal Mile, I think that I see them clearly, as if they were still there today:

Robert Burns, sharing a drink with friends in John Downie's pub in Libberton's Wynd; Allan Ramsay, busy with customers in his bookshop in Carrubber's Close; Old Playhouse Close and the bustle of the audience gathering for the first night of the scandalous play, *Douglas*; the painter Henry Raeburn, relaxing at the Isle of Man Tavern in Craig's Close off Cockburn Street.

Most of these men were educated at the Royal High School of Edinburgh, known as the "Tounis Scule". The story of Edinburgh is inextricably intertwined with that of the school, which traces its beginnings back to AD 1128 when King David I established the Abbey of Holyrood. I arrived at the school somewhat later, in 1943, and was a pupil there until 1954. My academic light shone less than brightly but I learned to love history, literature, art and music, and these joys have stayed with me throughout my life.

Whilst at Royal High, I also discovered the poetry of Robert Burns. There is a monument to him across the road from the old school on Calton Hill and each year on the anniversary of his birth, 25 January, senior pupils laid a wreath at this memorial. I won my only academic honour – well, nearly – by coming third in the annual competition for an essay on one of Burns' poems. From then on, I was determined to become a poet when I grew up. Still mean to when I grow up.

Burns arrived in Edinburgh in December 1786 with a "sair heed", caused by the generous hospitality he received from admirers along the way. He lodged with John Richmond, a friend from Mauchline who worked in the city, in a flat in Baxter's Close. The house has long since been demolished but the poet's residence there is commemorated in a plaque above the Lawnmarket entrance to Lady Stair's Close. Burns later lodged in Buccleuch Street with Willie Nicoll, a master at the High School, and he immortalized his friend in the lines:

Willie brew'd a peck o' maut'
And Rob and Allan cam to pree;

Three blyther hearts, that lee-lang night,
Ye wid na found in Christendie.

Burns was also a companion of the Crochallan Fencibles, a drinking club that met in Dawney Douglas's tavern in Anchor's Close. A product of these meetings was Burns' bawdy poems, later published as *The Merry Muses of Caledonia*, a copy of which is by my side as I write. It was during this visit that the poet met the young Walter Scott in a house in Braid Place, Sciennes, on the south side of the city. There is a plaque on the wall commemorating the meeting and I always used to make a detour, walking home from the Old Town to Newington where my parents lived, to read it.

Scott, a boy of fifteen at the time, later recalled: "There was a strong expression of sense and shrewdness in all his [Burns'] lineaments; the eye alone, I think, indicated the poetical character and temperament. It was large and of a dark cast, and glowed (I say literally glowed) when he spoke with feeling or interest. I never saw such another eye in a human head, though I have seen the most distinguished men of my time. His conversation expressed perfect self-confidence, without the slightest presumption."

On his second visit to Edinburgh in 1788, Burns lodged with another High School master, William Cruikshank, in St James's Square. St James's Square was wantonly demolished in the 1960s to make way for a shopping mall. On this visit, Burns began his ultimately fruitless relationship with his "Clarinda", Mrs James (Nancy) Maclehose. As an old woman, Nancy is said to have "spoke o' her love for the poet like a hellcat bit lassie in her teens. Whilst exhibiting to her cronies the faded letters from her Robbie, she would greet (cry) just like a bairn".

The best way to discover Edinburgh is on foot. As a boy, I used to roam the streets of the city. I haunted the Royal Mile, peering in windows, exploring the narrow wynds, climbing Arthur's Seat and Calton Hill to view the town and the surrounding hills, the broad blue sweep of the Firth of Forth, the distant mountains to the north. Time was a friend then, just the space between my dreams and dinner.

In my wanderings, I discovered the house in York Place where Henry Raeburn had his studio and I thought of him there, hard at work on his famous portrait of the Reverend Robert Walker skating on Duddingston Loch; the house where Robert Louis Stevenson stayed, 17 Heriot Row, and their family cottage in the village of Swanson on the edge of the Pentland Hills.

The walk from Cramond along the shore of the Firth of Forth to South Queensferry led me to the Hawes Inn, crouched below the massive bulk of the Forth Railway Bridge. Stevenson was a frequent visitor and he devised the plot of his book *Kidnapped* whilst staying in Room 13. Not so many years ago, I found myself in the same room, warmed by an open fire as Stevenson must have been. In his memory, I recited lines from one of his *Songs of Travel*:

> Spring shall come, come again, calling up the moor-fowl,
> Spring shall bring the sun and rain, bring the bees and flowers;
> Red shall the heather bloom over hill and valley,
> Soft flow the stream through the even-flowing hours;
> Fair the day shine as it shone on my childhood –
> Fair shine the day on the house with open door;
> Birds come and cry there and twitter in the chimney –
> But I go forever and come this way no more.

Another of my Edinburgh literary heroes is the poet Norman MacCaig who died in Edinburgh in 1996. My greatest regret is that I never worked up sufficient courage to go and meet him. We had much in common, both having been educated at the Royal High School, and both with a shared love of the broken lands of Assynt in Sutherland, stalking the hills there, fishing for wild brown trout. MacCaig's poetry echoes this love in its directness and does the work of Robert Burns, yet points the way forward to an as yet unseen, better world. Here is his poem, "Bell Heather":